PENNY POWER

True, Sequential and Humorous Stories about

How the Author Parlayed A

$100.00 CASH RETIREMENT GIFT

INTO OVER $50,000.00 CASH

Including examples of how to

HAVE JUST ABOUT ANY MATERIALISTIC THING THAT

ONE COULD WANT OR NEED - ABSOLUTELY FREE!

Copies of this book can be ordered from the Printer's Website,

www.lulu.com

Cover photograph by Betty Turpin

ISBN 978-0-6152-0941-8

Library of Congress Control Number: 2008904396

Dedication

This book is dedicated to my many friends and former co-workers of the Lake County, Florida Public School System; and especially to those who so generously donated to my one hundred dollars cash retirement gift.

And

To Betty, my most avid supporter, fan, best lifelong friend, partner, and loving wife. My special thanks to her for sharing with me her knowledge and skills as a certified and experienced Librarian and Media Specialist. This book would not have been the same without her editing, input, suggestions, and support with the process of ensuring that all my life's projects have a positive outcome.

Contents

INTRODUCTION

If you were to ask me to describe what this book is about with only one word, I would have to say "business." However, if I were allotted more than one word to do so, I would have to respond in a less formal manner by saying, "Horse-sense about horse-trading."

Penny Power is a series of chronological true stories about how I parlayed a $100.00 cash retirement gift into over $50,000.00 by applying the basic principles of business that I have learned from my experiences down through the years. No employees, no payroll taxes, no vehicles, no utilities, no warehouses, no offices, no inventory with a short shelf life, nor any of the other pitfalls that causes businesses to fail; just $100.00 cash, classified ads, my computer, and my cell phone. It is also about the thrill of owning and enjoying just about any possible materialistic thing that one could possible dream of; and how to do so absolutely free while making a profit in the process.

In order to be successful in business, the few basic principles that are demonstrated in this book must be applied, no matter whether you are working on a hundred dollar deal or a million dollar deal. People share the same emotions regardless of the size of the deal. If what I did is something that you would like to do, then just follow in my detailed footsteps and you should be able to do the same.

If you are one who enjoys the thrill of consummating an exciting and profitable business deal, whether it is small or large, read on because you will love this book. I will share with you some down-to-earth business tactics that you won't have to learn the hard way; and, that are probably not taught in business schools. On the other hand, if you are one that just likes to read about some true life experiences and interesting interactions between people with various backgrounds, then you too will really enjoy this book. Believe me, a lot of people take on a completely different personality when you are dealing with their money and their desire for "stuff."

Being in business for one's self is truly a unique experience. A lot of people will claim to have business experience when in fact, the closest that they have ever come to such a challenging phenomenon is to work for someone else who is a business person. Unfortunately, one such "spin-doctor" I know, whom I like to refer to as "the bobbing dog," was elected to head one of our large governmental agencies by claiming, among other things, that he would operate the system like a "business" based on his "business experience;" when in fact, about the closest he ever came to being a business person was working as a part-time employee at a local tourist attraction during the summers when school was not in session. And by the way, it was just a matter of time before the state "got rid of" him. Believe me when I say that a person who simply works in a business is not a business person and therefore, and in my opinion, has little or no true business experience. In case you are wondering whether or not you might be a business person, here are a few pointers that might help you with answering that question. If you receive a regular paycheck, you probably are not a business person. If someone else pays your health insurance, you probably are not a business person. If you get a vacation, you probably are not a business person. If you have a boss, other than the person from whom you buy or sell stuff or a service, you probably are not a business person. If you have a set time to be at work and a set time to leave work, you probably are not a business person. If you have never had a key employee walk off the job during your busiest part of the day, you probably are not a business person. If you have never sat up in your bed, in a cold sweat, at two-thirty in the morning in anguish about how you were going to meet a payroll, you probably are not a business person. If you have never been suited by a disgruntled and incompetent business associate or employee, you probably are not a business person. If you have never experienced a severe shortage of the stuff that you are selling, you probably are not a business person. If you have time to keep your toenails properly trimmed, you probably are not a business person. A real business person will just say, "I will trim them as soon as I can get around to it." The problem for any business person is finding that illusive "round toit" for such non-business related activities.

A business person is one who goes out in the cold, cold world without a job or any income, whatsoever, and makes it on his own. I always like to begin the process of measuring one's success by first determining where he or she started. I have been there so therefore I know. I started as a soldier in Germany. At the time, I had a wife and small child to support. Now when I say I was broke, I mean, I was broke! I did not have enough money to buy milk for our baby, so I went next door and borrowed enough from a complete stranger to buy a quart. I am telling you this true story to simply demonstrate that a lack of success cannot be attributed to not having any money to "get started on;" an excuse that I have heard many times. I have been told that "You are the luckiest person I have ever known." Yea, right, the smarter I work the luckier I get; now notice that I said "smarter," not "harder." I don't know for sure, but perhaps the situation of not having enough money to buy some milk for our baby has, at least in some way, influenced me to demonstrate what can be done with just $100.00. I have recorded my success in the form of this book. I could go on and on with this subject but I believe that you get the point that this book is about a series of successful business deals made by a real and experienced businessman.

My friends asked me a lot of questions while I was writing this book. As examples, "What is it about," and "Now that you have retired, are financially independent, and can do just about anything that you want to do, why in the world would you want to take on such a project; much less write a book about it?" I answer by saying that it is about the business principles that I have learned the hard way down through the years. That I am taking on such a project because, that to the best of my knowledge, it has never before been done this way. That it provides me with a way to demonstrate the success of proven business principles and practices. I am thankful that I now have the income and time for such a project. To those who say, "But you are old," I respond by asking, "How many young people do you know who have the business experience to write a book like this?" And by the way, unlike some people who have retired but continue to work in order to buy more stuff, I am doing what I want to do. I believe that there comes a time in life when it becomes important to stop planting more crops; and instead, enjoy the harvest of others that have been planted before they die in the field. In other words, try to time it so that the last check that you write before you die "bounces."

I have met a lot of dreamer's in my lifetime but fewer doers. One must be both if he is to ever see his dreams come true. There are many self-made millionaires out there with almost as many different ways to become one. My project, as recorded in this book, was to demonstrate only one simple way that it can be done. I am thankful that the founding fathers of our great country have provided us with such unlimited opportunities for personal success. Yea, I know, all this sounds "corny." Just lighten up and enjoy, because in this case, it just happens to be true!

CHAPTER ONE

($100.00 doubled only 9 times equals $51,200.00)

The Amazing Power of Exponential Growth

A lot of people get a big kick out of putting a ball into a hole, a basket, or some other place of unimportance. I honestly couldn't care less about a ball, much less where it goes; especially if someone else is putting it there. So, it goes in the hole, so what? I know, I know, it takes skill, right? In my opinion, one's most insignificant activity surely must be watching grown men playing with a ball. To me, the outcome of a ball game is only a grain of sand in the great dune of life. Anyway, if sports or chasing a ball is your thing, then go for it. Life is too short to not enjoy it. Personally I get the greatest amount of satisfaction from a successful business deal. Not only is it challenging, it has a very tangible, useful and measurable result. I never have to be concerned about putting business before pleasure because for me, business is pleasure. I much prefer receiving a few thousand dollars profit on a successful business deal than a cheap trophy for putting a ball in a hole. The above title for this chapter contains an example of a very simple formula that can be used to make you rich. Let us suppose that we start with $100.00 as the first listed amount in the title and that the last listed amount is also in dollars. Hadn't you really rather turn $100.00 into $51,200.00 cash, as I did and have explained in this book, than watch someone use a stick to knock a ball in a little hole? Well, enough of this or my sport fan friends won't like me much any more.

Now that you know that successful business is the sporting force that drives me, I want to share with you some of the exciting business ventures that permitted me to turn a $100.00 retirement gift into $50,000.00; plus several hundred dollars as a matter of fact. If this sounds like an exiting journey that you would like to take yourself, then read on. You should be able to easily follow the same steps and accomplish the same goal for yourself. If you can come up with $100.00, have the desire, and apply the business principles that you can learn from my experiences, you too can earn a lot of money and have just about any materialistic thing that you want.

The most valuable advice that you can get is from someone who has already successfully been where you want to go. Such a person can provide you with the mile marker numbers that will lead you to your destination. I believe you will find that in most business schools, business tactics are taught by a professor who was taught by a professor who was taught by a professor. I call this "educational inbreeding." More than likely, none of them have even "been there," much less "done that." This statement might sound as if it is coming from an uneducated person that is being defensive. Now before my educator friends get too up in the air about this, let me say that you can believe me when I tell you that this is not the case. I am educated and I do support education to the fullest extent possible. Education has opened the doors of success for a lot of people like me who would not have otherwise had the opportunity to succeed. As a matter of fact, education has been one of my major career paths. I hold a Bachelor of Science Degree from a very highly respected university, a Master of Science Degree from the same university, plus a certificate in Leadership and Administration from one of the top state universities in the country. Although throughout my life I have applied many of the basic business principles in which I believe, my education provided me with the opportunity to progress from a military officer, to part-time school teacher, to full-time school teacher, to school Principal, to District Administrator, to Director of Facilities, and finally to District Assistant Superintendent for Business, Finance and Support Services of a very large public school district. I am proud of the fact that all of this was accomplished in only ten years. The last two years of my career in education were at the highest in the education profession without entering the world of politics. In our school district, the Superintendent of Schools is an elected position and I have never had a desire to become personally involved in politics.

In my opinion, an educator enters into a whole new career path when he or she becomes a politician. My major areas of responsibility, for the entire Florida school district of approximately 40,000 students and an annual budget of approximately 250 million dollars, were budgeting and finance, facility maintenance and new construction, student transportation, food service, technology, management information services, and risk management. We, the district staff, the school board and the citizens' advisory committee working as a team, transformed a large school district in a financial crisis of near bankruptcy to one with sufficient finances for major remodeling, renovation and new construction projects throughout the district; and at the same time, generated over a nine-million dollar unreserved fund balance.

A former Superintendent of Schools to whom I was responsible wrote in a statement, among other appreciated accolades, that "A recent performance report included savings of more than $50 million in cost reductions in the school facilities designs for which Mr. Turpin is responsible." Although I am proud of the fact that I was able to save the taxpayers that amount of money in only one year, I am really sharing all this information with you because I want to emphasize my belief in the importance of education and to provide you with some evidence to support the business related statements that I will be making later on. As you have probably concluded by now, I am trying to give credibility to the contents of this book. I honestly believe that you will place more value on what I have to say if you are aware of some of the places where I have been and some of the things that I have done.

13

By the way, did you ever think about how ridiculous it is for a man to wear a "suit and tie" as I had to do for many years? Now think about this subject for a minute; first off, we put on an undershirt. Then we stick our arms into a long-sleeved white shirt and dare not get anything of a dark-colored substance on it; and of course most of such gooey substances are of a dark color aren't they? Then after the underwear and a pair of wool paints are pulled up around our waist and drawn tight with a strong leather belt, we proceed to wrap a strip of tough cloth, know as a "tie," tightly around our neck; you think that this might be the reason it is called a tie? And oh yes, we must tie it tight because if we don't, a little air might accidentally seep in around the neck area and keep us a little cool.

Now just in case a button or two were to melt off the front of the ole white shirt due to excessive heat, also resulting in a little cool air reaching our body, we must be prepared to stop up a hole. To do this, a safety measure in the form of a tightly buttoned-up vest is worn over the shirt. And oh yea, we must not forget to fasten the three buttons on the shirt sleeves as tightly as possible for the same reason. Boy there is a real safety measure for you; as many as two buttons can melt off a sleeve but we still have the one to keep us from getting any dangerous cool air up the arm.

I bet that you can guess what is next; the coat! Yes, a long-sleeved wool coat to match the paints; and I emphasize the "wool" part of this. Why do you suppose we wear such a hot thing? Well I've got the answer for you; sweat! We can't afford to let anyone see us sweat so the tightly closed dark-colored coat is worn to hide the sweaty shirt. I really believe that some Eskimo came up with such a dress code and over time, some Florida "cracker" thought that it looked "cool;" now there is a play on words for you. And by the way, I, like many other poor withered souls, had to wear such miserable bindings while living and working in Florida where the summer temperatures during the days average around the 100 degrees mark. I thought that you just might like to know my thoughts on this subject; meanwhile, let's return to the business at hand.

I am the son of an entrepreneur who was the son of an entrepreneur. My grandfather started a lumber company and construction business in 1889 and the passion has articulated down through the generations. I probably had one of the greatest and hardest working dads in the whole world, but he "spent as he went" like most people do today. He made a lot of money in his lifetime but was not able to parlay any part of it into financial independence for retirement. As a matter of fact, he not only died a broke man at the age of 64, he left a rather large debt for his family to deal with. At that time, I vowed to myself that I would not let this happen to me; that I would learn how to use a small amount of money as a tool to make more money, and eventually, lead to a future that would permit me the time to enjoy the many pleasures of life; such as writing this book. Now hang in there with me because I am going to explain how I did it as we go along my entrepreneurial journey.

I have always considered a business as being similar to an item that is bought, polished up a bit, and then resold for a profit. A lot of my friends and acquaintances have, from time to time, said that I was very unpredictable because I didn't "stick with" anything for a very long period of time. But what they didn't, and probably still don't, realize is that there is a great deal of pleasure as well as profit to be realized from starting a business, grooming its growth, and then selling it as an established firm. Likewise, there is an equal amount of satisfaction to be gained from buying a business, correcting some deficiencies, and then reselling it for a profit; or perhaps continuing to operate it as an ongoing source of income. However, I believe that this is a good point in time to explain to you one of my very basic business beliefs. I strongly believe that if one has a real good profitable business, he should sell it before it goes bad; because it will more than likely go bad, it is just a matter of time. Now think about what I have just said for a moment and try to remember some of the businesses that you used to patronize that are no longer in business. Time and new developments change people's habits and desires. Times changed and my dad's business went bad before his own eyes. He wasn't able to prevent it from happening, no matter how hard he tried. He owned and operated a building supply business when the large retailers, such as Lowe's and Home Depot, began to emerge on the scene. He could not compete and no longer had a business that he could operate or sell for any reasonable price.

Without knowing it, my dad taught me a very valuable business lesson. You might think that I would not want to own any business after witnessing his business experience, but such thoughts would be wrong. As a matter of fact, I have either started or purchased several businesses since then; including mobile home sales and service, a chain of bicycle stores, used car business, fine jewelry stores, a real estate and auction business, an auction school, subdivision development, construction business, and even a well-known franchised fried chicken restaurant. I am happy to report that all of them were operated at a profit and all subsequently sold for a profit. Therefore, if you are considering buying or starting a business, don't let the outcome of my dad's experience discourage you.

Now then, let me share with you the single most important basic fact that I have learned from all of my business experiences; the most, and easiest, money is to be made from buying and selling something. This point is so important that it deserves to be repeated; the most, and easiest, money is to be made from buying and selling something; period! Consider Wal-Mart, Home Depot, Sears, and even your local Chevrolet dealer as examples; isn't that exactly what they do on a large scale? My purpose for writing this book was to prove this point by using my $100.00 cash retirement gift to buy "something" that I could resell for a profit, and then keep re-investing the profits utilizing the business principles that I have learned in life. In each of the succeeding chapters, I will describe, in detail, the adventures, the fun and the interesting interactions of people that I have enjoyed along the way. Keep in mind that I accomplished my goal without the need for employees, retail space, equipment, large startup capital, utilities, storage room, or any other of the expensive needs that are normally associated with a business. All I used was my calculator, computer and pen for signing contracts; plus of course my pickup truck for transportation.

I believe that now is an excellent opportunity for me to ensure that we are communicating on the subjects of "goal" and "objective." In the process of discussing these two subjects, I have learned that those involved frequently do not have a mutual understanding of their meanings. My purpose here is not to attempt to educate the world in this matter; I only want to make sure that you understand what I mean when I use the terms. Personally, I use a comparative to help me with the terminology. For example, a war has only one "goal;" and that is to win. To do so, a series of battles have to be won. I like to refer to the battles as "objectives" along the way to winning. In comparison, my goal was to earn a minimum of $50,000.00 on my $100.00 cash gift. I refer to the steps that I took to accomplish my goal as objectives, each of which is represented in the sequential chapters of this book. I bet that we are now on the same page; literally and figurative.

In each of the following chapters, I will emphasize some of the major business principles that I have developed or learned down through the years; and as a former educator, hope that you will value each principle as a separate and valuable lesson while traveling your adventurous road to financial success.

I am sure that my retirement gift was similar to those that others receive from colleagues when retiring. The big difference in my case was the fact that I had been working with them in their school district for only two years. Before then, they were all strangers to me. This fact makes me even more appreciative of the $100.00 gift. On the day of my retirement, the school district's Assistant Superintendent for Curriculum, Mr. Jim Polk, told me that he and "some of the boys" would like to take me to lunch. By then, Jim had become a very close and dependable friend as well as an admired and respected colleague. Anyway, Jim and about a half dozen of the "guys" took me to one of our favorite restaurants at the time. Maybe it is because of our southern raising, but we both really did like the fried chicken there. The breading was always crispy and cooked to perfection. Having been in the fried chicken business, I believe that it was also good because it was freshly cooked. After a good meal and about a dozen good jokes and stories had been told, Jim got serious about the occasion and presented me with a very well worded retirement card, inside of which, was a one-hundred dollar bill. Now I don't know about you, but a crisp hundred-dollar bill will get my attention over a crisp piece of chicken any day. The card included best wishes and the signatures of 86 people representing fellow employees, School Board members and others associated with the school district office. I was especially impressed with the large number of well-wishers, especially considering the fact that I was a relatively newcomer to the district. To all of you in the Lake County School District, thank you! I deeply appreciate your friendship, your gift and your inspiration for me to write this book.

One of the most fascinating principles of business, and the main theme of this book, is the one dealing with "exponential growth." The dictionary describes exponential as, "A mathematical function that contains an independent variable used as an exponent." How is that for a brain twister? Probably written by a professor, huh? Now let me tell you in my terms what exponential growth means; exponential growth means that instead of spending your penny, you let it multiply to earn more pennies for you. Keep this up until you convert your pennies into thousands of dollars.

What I am going to demonstrate now about exponential growth will really pop your corn. Let us say that you have a job that you would like to get done and it sure would be nice to hire someone to do it for you.   Perhaps the job will take a month, maybe no more than 31 days. I hope that you are ready for this because I am about to make you an offer that you can't refuse. I will personally come to work for you for the 31 days for only one penny the first day; that is, if you will double the penny every day for the 31 days. Now before you send out an all-points bulletin to find me, you need to read on to become aware of the bottom line cost to which you are about to commit. This is how it shapes up:

Cost for day 1: Only one cent

Cost for day 2: One cent x 2 = two cents

Cost for day 3: Two cents x 2 = four cents

Cost for day 4: Four cents x 2 = eight cents

Cost for day 5: Eight cents x 2 = sixteen cents

Five whole days of work for a total of only 31 cents! Not bad for you, huh? You sure would get your money's worth out of me the first workweek.   Hang on for a minute now and take a look at your cost for the rest of the 31 days:

Cost for day 6: Sixteen cents x 2 = 32 cents

Cost for day 7: Thirty-two cents x 2 = 64 cents

Cost for day 8: Sixty-four cents x 2 = $1.28

Cost for day 9: $1.28 x 2 = $2.56

You might have noticed that by now I have gone from "cents" to using the ole "dollar" sign. By the way, I have now turned on my calculator because I am beginning to need it:

Cost for day 10: $2.56 x 2 = $5.12

Cost for day 11: $5.12 x 2 = $10.24

Cost for day 12: $10.24 x 2 = $20.48

Cost for day 13: $20.48 x 2 = $40.96

Cost for day 14: $40.96 x 2 = $81.92

Cost for day 15: $81.92 x 2 = $163.84

Cost for day 16: $163.84 x 2 = $327.68

Ok, we have now passed the half-way mark of the 31 days and your total cost for 16 days of productive work has been only $655.35, for an average of $40.96 per day. Now if only you could get me to work the remainder of the 31 days for this daily average, you would really be getting a good deal. But, that is not what we agreed to, right? As a matter of fact, it wasn't, so you therefore have to continue the pattern of exponential growth, as follows:

Cost for day 17: $327.68 x 2 = $655.36

Cost for day 18: $655.36 x 2 = $1,310.72

Oh my goodness, we are now up to over a thousand dollars per day, but it gets better; for me that is, not you. Look what happens now:

Cost for day 19: $1,310.72 x 2 = $2,621.44

Cost for day 20: $2,621.44 x 2 = $5,242.88

Cost for day 21: $5,242.88 x 2 = $10,485.76

Cost for day 22: $10,485.76 x 2 = $20,971.52

Cost for day 23: $20,971.52 x 2 = $41,943.04

Cost for day 24: $41,943.04 x 2 = $83,886.08

Cost for day 25: $83,886.08 x 2 = $167,772.16

Cost for day 26: $167,772.16 x 2 = $335,544.32

Cost for day 27: $335,544.32 x 2 = $671,088.64

Cost for day 28: $671,088.64 x 2 = $1,342,177.28

Cost for day 29: $1,342,177.28 x 2 = $2,684,354.56

Cost for day 30: $2,684,354.56 x 2 = $5,368,709.12

Cost for day 31: $5,368,709.12 x 2 = $10,737,418.24

Now, when we add up all the daily costs, our total for the 31 days is $18,789,826.56. No, this is not a misprint; it comes to almost nineteen million dollars. See what I mean? The dollars start to multiply faster than rabbits at a 6-month hare convention. By now any of you doubters out there must surely believe me when I again say, do not spend a penny! Let us say for example that after the 18th day, I spent my $1,310.00 that I had earned to that date. I would had to start all over again, a move that would have cost me a total of $18,788,515.00 (yes, almost nineteen million dollars). I'm sure that there will be some mathematical experts out there that will tell me that I didn't have to go into so much detail to make this all-important point. My response will be, "oh yes I did, because it is hard for average folk like me to comprehend the overwhelming impact of exponential growth without seeing it demonstrated."

I would like to tell you another little true story about the impact of exponential growth, the deals of which are not included in this book, and then I will get off the subject for now. About 15 years ago, I looked down the road to retirement and didn't see much income at the end of it. With the memory of my dad's financial situation later in his life, I decided that I needed to do something about that fearful conclusion in my case. I thought about the penny-a-day concept and decided to apply it to real estate; more specifically, rental property. I had learned a lot about the developing and construction businesses in my lifetime and therefore decided to design and build my own rental houses, to my specifications, for the purpose of having a renewable monthly income during my old age. I told Betty that I wanted to find a small lot in a nice section of our city, buy it and save up enough money to build a rental house on it. She agreed and we both started saving a much as we could from our paychecks. When we had accumulated enough funds to pay for the materials, I began work. I finished the house and rented it without having to borrow a single dime. Over a period of time, we saved the income from that first rental and continued to save as much from our paychecks as we could. After about 2 ½ years, we had enough money to build our second rental house. Remember the impact of exponential growth? We then had the income from two rental houses in addition to what we continued to save from our paychecks. Yes, you guessed it; we didn't have to wait 2 ½ more years to start our third house. We built our fourth and fifth houses after only a few years. Pretty soon we were building a house per year and paying for it before it was finished. This led to house numbers 7, 8, etc (I won't say how more at this time); all in a great section of the city, all paid for, all almost new, and all rented. Instead of spending our income on interest, we were able to invest 100% of it in more properties (we did not spend a penny of the income). I learned a long time ago that bankers make a lot of money by loaning other people money. If you have any doubt about this, just check out who owns the fanciest and biggest buildings in town, all of which are paid for by the average person that doesn't think that there is anyway to buy what they want without borrowing money from a bank and making payments on the loan over a period of many years. Interest costs usually end up costing more than whatever it was that they purchased; which by the way, is probably worn out before it is paid for. Well, enough on this subject for now. Perhaps those experiences of finding lots, designing and building houses, and effectively dealing with tenants will be the subject of a future book of interest to you.

In summary of this subject, I truly do believe that a proper application of the exponential growth principle can make a poor person financially independent beyond his wildest dreams, especially if the process is begun at an early age. If others have done it, so can you!

CHAPTER TWO

What to Buy Is the Big Question

Armed with the knowledge of business that I had gained from my previous experiences, and a crisp one hundred dollar bill, I set myself on a course of parlaying my $100.00 retirement gift into $50,000.00. Remember what I said before about buying and selling something? It is the easiest way to make money. What to buy, what to buy – that was the important question at this stage of my project. In other words, in what kind of "stuff" was I going to deal? I explored several categories in search of the ideal classification.

In the beginning of my search, it occurred to me that the classified ads in most newspapers consisted of numerous categories, so I decided to begin my search there. I was really surprised to find that the morning edition of our local newspaper listed a total of 316 classifications in their classified ads; everything from baby bottles to buses. The first category, "Notices," contained 50 classifications. I eliminated all of these right away because I new that I wasn't likely to make much money buying and reselling any kind of notice.

The second category was "Employment." I assumed that an employment agency could possibly be a profitable business, but it is was not something that captured my interest. I will leave the task of finding a job for other people up to the government; besides, I don't have any desire to compete with taxpayer's employment offices. Discarding this category eliminated an additional 33 classifications from my future list of stuff to buy for resale.

The next two categories contained classifications in the area of real estate. The first of the two was "Rentals." I didn't consider the rental category as being in the stuff family, so the 36 classifications there were tossed out. The second of these two categories was simply named, "Real Estate." Now there is some stuff for you; classifications of everything from residential lots to ranches. Maybe too big of an investment required at this stage of my project, but some interesting classifications for later consideration. Although real estate was, and still is, an area of great interest to me, many of the classifications, such as "Real Estate Maps," were eliminated. Of the 46 real estate classifications, only 15 remained as good possibilities. Those that did remain consisted of single and multiple-family homes, lots, acreage, commercial, condos, and other types of properties. I also included mobile homes and manufactured housing classifications in the category of real estate because they are so closely related. There certainly are many opportunities around this great country of ours for buying and selling real estate for a profit. If you have any doubt about this statement, check out Donald Trump's holdings (no, not Turpin, Trump). And of course, you are welcome to also check out my holdings in real estate.

The "Business" category included 14 classifications. The only one of those that I found of interest was "Businesses for Sale." However, I was reluctant to even include the classification. I have learned that businesses are generally very difficult to sell, and even harder for a buyer to get financed. To help consolidate my list of possibilities, I included this classification under the category of real estate. After all, they too are usually closely related. I concluded that perhaps, but not likely, someday I might be able to buy a business with a lot of stuff that I could resell for a nice profit. After all, it has been reported that at least 90% of all new businesses go broke sometime during the first six years of operation. Those are not the kind of odds that I prefer to play around with.

Next on the list of categories was "Merchandise." At first I thought, oh boy, lots of stuff here for sure! A whopping 79 classifications had been listed there. However, a closer analysis revealed that only a very few of those appealed to me as being possibilities for consideration. As a matter of fact, "Lawn and Garden" and "Machinery and Tools" were the only two classifications in the category that I found to be of interest. You might be thinking, "How can that be when there are 77 others to consider?" Well that is a good question and I believe that it needs to be addressed here by providing you with a summary of my conclusions.

I consider the areas of tools, machinery and equipment to contain many items that can be bought and resold for a profit. However, like all other classifications, I always appreciate the importance of having a good working knowledge of

27

whatever it is in which I am dealing. I found this to be especially true of values. This leads me to some of the reasons why I eliminated the 77 classifications under the category of merchandise. I will use a few of the classifications to summarize my point. Let us consider "antiques" for example. Dealing in antiques can be a very profitable business; that is, if you know a lot about antiques, which I don't. I do know however, that it would be very easy for a dishonest person to take advantage of me when it comes to antiques. Although I was an auctioneer of antiques for several years, I believe that staying clear of the antique classification is certainly in my best interest.

For the next example, let's consider the classifications of "Appliances." I don't know about you, but I don't have any desire to spend my time lifting, hauling, storing, and fixing old and dirty refrigerators, ranges, washers, and dryers. I especially dislike the "fixing" part of the idea. After all, used appliances are usually worn out; otherwise they would not be for sale. For the same reasons, I eliminated the category of "Electronics."

I am not a farmer and know very little about the values of "Fruits and Vegetables." But I do know for a fact that my big concern with this classification would be "shelf-life." This brought a lot of other concerns to mind; for example, how much could I sell before it spoils? Without knowing the answer to that question, I wouldn't know how much to buy would I. Another major concern that I had about this classification was competition. I concluded that when one farmer's tomato crop was ripe, so are all the others in the neighborhood. And of course, this does not include the thrifty housewife down the street that raises her own vegetables in her backyard, and therefore has no reason to buy mine at any price. I promise to leave all the fruit and vegetable farming to real farmers if they in return will stay out of the real estate business.

Two other classifications that I immediately eliminated were "Pets" and "Farm Animals." I will tell you right up front, if it eat and poops, I don't want anything to do with it. I am not at all interested in spending money for food to feed an animal, and I am less interested in cleaning up its manure after the food has served its purpose. But of course, farmers have the expertise and resources for the possibility of a profitable business in buying and reselling animals; and perhaps making a profit off their poop.

I discovered that there are at least six classifications in the category of "Recreation" that provide excellent "farming" for stuff to buy for resell. They are bicycles, recreational vehicles, campers, fishing equipment, guns, and golfing equipment. There are several laws, that vary from one geographical location to another, pertaining to many of these items. For example, a license is required to deal in guns. Therefore, I chose to not include that classification in my list. Besides, I'm not fond of the possibility of getting shot.

In my opinion, the categories of "Boating" and "Transportation" contain the best gold mines after that of real estate. There are numerous opportunities for profit in both, especially in the state of Florida. Boating includes the classifications of all types of boats, motors, trailers, personal watercraft, kayaks, and canoes. I targeted 10 classifications to pursue in the boating category. The "Transportation" category provided even a larger selection of possibilities.

Although there were 14 classifications in that category to explore, they could be consolidated into six major areas: aviation, motorcycles, trailers, automobiles, trucks, vans, and commercial vehicles. One major plus for dealing in these classifications is the fact that the values can be easily determined by referring to one of the reputable guides available on the internet.

After considering all the above bits and pieces of information, I made a list of the categories of "stuff" in which I would perform my "wheeling-and-dealing." That list included the following:

Real Estate (including Mobile Homes and Manufactured Housing)

Lawn and Garden Tools and Equipment

Other Tools, Machinery and Equipment

Recreation

Boating

Transportation

A lot of time can be saved by concentrating the search to these six categories for stuff to buy for resale. I am convinced that my opportunities for a profit in buying and reselling stuff are limited only by the time that I have to invest.

I have also learned to further narrow my search when considering what to buy for resale. I do so by ensuring that the item or property being considered passes my "PAD" test. I cannot overemphasize the importance of making sure that the project is:

1. Popular: it must be used, worn, driven, ridden, or at least acceptable by a minimum of 50% of the general population.

2. Affordable: at least 50% of the general population must be able to afford it.

3. Desirable: the item must be such that it is desired by at least 50% of the general population.

I have no doubt that by now you have concluded that my "yardstick" is the "at least 50% of the general population" requirement. As an example, let's apply the test to an automobile that is being considered as a project. First of all, it must be a brand, color, size, type transmission, etc. that is seen most often on the road. In other words, it must be "popular." A Chevrolet that is white, small in size so that it gets good gas mileage, and has an automatic transmission is popular. Going a little to the extreme to make my point, you would probably have a very difficult time selling a Mercedes that is bright florescent orange in color, the size of a "stretch" limousine, has a standard shift transmission, and is powered by a 5,000 horsepower jet engine that gets 1/2 mile per gallon of fuel; even if you could buy such an awful looking thing for $100.00 or less.

It must be in a price range that is "affordable" by over 50% of the average working class citizens. I'm not sure what the average cost of a used car is, but I estimate it to be somewhere in the $8,000.00 range. Anytime that the price is much lower, the car probably is not very popular; likewise, if it is priced much higher, the average person cannot afford it.

Now let's put the "desirable" part of my test to the test; so to speak. Still using an automobile as an example, it must also be one that is desired by most of the same category of people. A late model car that passes the first two parts of my test but has 150,000 miles on it would be hard to resell. Therefore, before I will buy a car to resell, or any other type of vehicle as a matter of fact, it absolutely must have fewer miles on it than the average in the category. If the item or property passes my PAB test, and is reasonably priced of course, you can bet on it selling fast because it will appeal to, and be desired by, a lot of people who can afford it.

CHAPTER THREE

Beginning with Bicycles

Now are you ready for this? I bought two bicycles for $50.00 each! That's right, two bicycles. This is a great first story that I will use to demonstrate the importance of one of my basic business tactics in negotiating; avoid debating value with the seller.

I am an early riser and enjoy reading the local newspaper while having a cup of coffee about 5:30 in the morning. While perusing the classified ads, I came across the following advertisement under the heading of "Bicycle Sales/Repair:"

"BIKES – 2 folding, used twice, paid over $200 each. $85.00 each obo…"

I thought to myself, now here is an opportunity to double my $100.00. If I could negotiate to buy them for $50.00 each, I would shore up my chances of doubling my investment, as a minimum. I called the seller and inquired about the location of the bikes and when it would be convenient for me to come see them. He gave me the address, which is in one of the area's retirement communities. I concluded that the owner was an older gentlemen who probably wanted to "get rid of" the bikes because he was too old to ride them anymore. I also assumed that the bikes must be in good condition because he told me that he had always kept them in his garage. Also, if he was telling me the truth that they had been ridden only twice, they must be in a like-new condition.

Betty and I do a lot of traveling in our motorcoach, and as a result, have seen several of these type folding bicycles being ridden in campgrounds around the country. I believed that they could easily be resold by advertising them in a section of the classifieds that appeals to camping enthusiasts. It is very important to target a group of prospective buyers before purchasing anything. I will discuss this subject in more detail when we get to the chapter about one of my real estate deals. Before responding to the ad, I checked one of my RV catalogs and learned that the new cost of one of the bicycles was $225.00. A good bit of advice here is to always learn the current value of the items or items that you might buy before beginning any negotiations to buy them.

I made an appointment to see the bicycles at 10:00 A.M. It was a beautiful sunny Saturday morning and the 15-mile ride in my pickup was very enjoyable. The development in which the seller lived is what is known around here as a "gated community." When I arrived at the front gate, the guard in the guard's shack greeted me with arrogance and a strong impression that he believed I was there to steal all the television sets, rape all the widows and otherwise create havoc amongst the peace and tranquility of the golf course. He obviously valued the importance of his job more than I. Anyway, after a few questions about my

34

intentions and a call to the seller's home, he gave me a map of the development and reluctantly showed me the way to my first purchase.

When I arrived at the home of the seller, the garage door was up and I could see the bikes sitting there as fresh and shiny as a pair of new pennies. An elderly gentleman and an elderly lady, obviously his wife, were standing in the garage and pretending to be unconcerned about my visit. It was obvious that they were anxiously awaiting my arrival and the opportunity to test their skills in the art of selling. The garage floor was painted a shiny gray color and the reflections of the bicycles shown upward as if they were on a mirror. They were obviously worth the seller's asking price. At that point, I made up my mind to buy both of them for resale even if I had to include a little of my own funds to do so. But, I also remained very determined to buy them for no more than $50.00 each.

I introduced myself and tried to avoid an immediate discussion about the real reason that I was there. This tends to downplay the importance of the item or items. I had never seen so many model airplanes in my life. They were on the garage floor, stacked on shelves and hanging from the ceiling. I got the impression that I was on a miniature air force base. After admiring his collection of model airplanes, I finally got around to the subject of the bicycles. The gentleman gave me a lengthy description of the bikes, told me what great condition they were in and explained why they were really worth the asking price. It was very important that I did not dispute him by trying to debate their worth. He was also correct in his explanation as to the condition of the bicycles and I did

35

not want to create an argument about that subject. Instead, I asked him if he would mind if I took a short ride on one of them. He said "not at all," of course. I rode to the street and back. The bicycle didn't seem to be very stable due to the looseness of the folding frame and the small size of the wheels. I immediately recognized these as negotiating points in my favor. I asked him if he had noticed these two minor problems with the bicycles. He, in all honesty, had to say that he had. I told him that I did not question the value of the bicycles and asked if they had received any offers on them. He said that they had not. I again told the gentleman that the bicycles could very well be worth what they were asking, but that I had only $100.00 to spend on two bicycles. I further added that they might get their asking price if they hold them long enough and show them to enough prospective buyers. I added that however, "I've got a hundred-dollar bill that I will give for them right now and take them off your hands." Now here is another important point to remember; the first person to speak after you make an offer will usually lose. I did not say another word and walked outside the garage to provide them with an opportunity to discuss my offer in private. After a couple of minutes, they told me that my offer was low, but that they would accept it. I gave them my hundred-dollar bill, loaded the bikes in my pickup and headed home with my first purchase.

The following Monday morning, I placed a "for sale" ad for them in the classifieds of our local newspaper. Instead of under the merchandise category of "Bicycles," I placed it under "Campers/Travel Trailers." My ad read:

"BICYCLES, RV, folding. Used only twice. Cost $225 each. 1st $275 for both..."

I priced the bikes with the notion that I could give a little on the price and still double my investment as a minimum. Remember this very important fact that I learned from being in the real estate business; in approximately 82% of the time, prospective buyers will either pay the asking price or walk away without making an offer lower than the asking price. To me, that means that most people do not like to negotiate. On the other hand, a few people enjoy negotiating and will not buy hardly anything unless they can buy it for less than the asking price. Now the trick here is to place yourself in a position to deal with both types of buyers. In other words, don't price anything so high that a real buyer will walk away from the deal. On the other hand, never price anything so low that you cannot give a little to accommodate the other 18% of prospective buyers.

I did not receive a single call on the bicycles during the first week that the ad ran. I was beginning to think that maybe I would have been better off if the guard so proudly perched in his shack had refused to admit me to the development. Betty and I took the bikes camping with us and used them around the campgrounds. Now here is a related point that is very valuable; I try to deal in something that I can use while it is on the market for sale. Now think about this a minute; you can literally have anything that you want for your personal use, and not only for free, but at a profit. Later on, in Chapter Sixteen, I will tell you a few interesting stories about this subject.

I got a call from a prospective buyer for the bicycles on the seventh day. The caller asked a lot of questions, which is always good because it shows a sincere interest. She wanted to know the least that I would take for them. It is important to not respond to that question with a "bottom dollar price." This told me that she was a member of the 18% group that liked to negotiate. I never reveal my "bottom price" because I do not want to eliminate my position to negotiate; and besides, if it is too high, the potential buyer will never come to see the item. Instead, I told the caller that I would like to suggest that she come see the bicycles, and if they were what she was looking for, she could make me an offer. She agreed and we set a time for her to come inspect them.

Upon arrival, and after the usual introductions, the lady began her effort to find fault with the bicycles and to tell me that they were not worth the price that I was asking. I just smiled and listened while deciding how I could use her desire to negotiate to my advantage. She finally said that the bicycles were not worth over $250.00. With the profit that I could realize at this point, it was very difficult to frown and tell her that she sure was a good negotiator, but that was exactly what I did. She immediately informed me that she was a real estate agent and that negotiating was her specialty. I told her that I sure was at a disadvantage, trying to negotiate with a professional like her, but that I really knew that the value of the bicycles was $275.00. After some hesitation, I told her that I would let her have them for $265.00. She again said that the bikes were not worth it, but that she would give $260.00 for them. This was the final negotiating. I let her negotiate me to only $160.00 profit on a $100.00 investment; shame on me. Not bad considering that I was up against a "professional." In my opinion, the lady was more concerned about her image as a negotiator than she was about the price that she was paying. The moral of this story is to never let your emotions override the importance of effectively negotiating. I really would have taken $200.00 for the bicycles because that amount would have permitted me to reach my objective. After only one deal, I then had $260.00 to reinvest. Not bad for a beginning, you agree? Stay with me now because it gets even better as my pennies continue to multiply.

CHAPTER FOUR

The Canoe and Other Stuff

It was about 6:00 AM on a beautiful Tuesday morning in April. The door to our verandah was open and the birds were already singing. The temperature in Ocala, Florida was at a pleasant 71 degrees and the smell of the season's first orange blossoms was in the air. Armed with my $260.00 from selling the two bicycles, I settled in with my first cup of coffee over our local newspaper and began my "hunt." I consider this to be just about as good as it gets. Why in the world would I want to go traipsing through some bug-infested woods hunting for a poor little innocent animal to shoot and kill when I can enjoy a hunt like this? If you now believe that my sport is hunting for deals, you are absolutely right. I have never been interested in hunting animals. I have always known that I can get my meat a lot easier and cheaper by buying it rather than hunting for it. Have you ever watched someone "field dress" an animal that they killed? Yuk, it is enough to break the average person from the habit of eating meat. I personally had rather hunt for money, but if hunting for animals is your thing, then you really need to work on improving that camouflage outfit because I can still see you! Anyway, back to the classifieds. Our local newspaper featured a daily section of new classified advertisements, called, "New Today." I really did like this section because I didn't have to waste time with the ads that I have already seen on previous days. Most of my deals, both buys and sales, have been made using the classifieds of newspapers and the internet. For you animal hunters out there, this is kind of like hunting rabbits with a helicopter.

When hunting for something to buy, I always check out the local classifieds first because if I find something of interest, I can be the first on the scene much faster than I can if the seller is in another area of the state. I am not very fond of clichés, but it seems to me that the one about "the early bird gets the worm," is very appropriate to use here. I know that if it is a good deal, I had better get there first or it will have already been sold. This means that you had better not wait until after 9:00 AM to make that inquiring phone call or some other bird will have the worm and gone. Instead, make that call not later than 8:00 AM. I recently purchased a pickup truck, which I found in the classifieds of course, for my personal use. I called about it at 7:15 AM and arrived at the seller's home at about 7:45 AM. Within 15 minutes after I arrived, there were two additional buyers, including a local mayor, in the driveway waiting to see if I was going to buy it or not. The truck had only 12,000 miles on it and was a good deal at the asking price. I knew right away that the seller was not in a position to bargain with me when he had two other buyers waiting, so I fought my natural instinct to negotiate and told him that I would take it. This reminds me of another good business principal in addition to going to buy with knowledge of the item's value; and that is, try to recognize a good deal when you see it and don't hesitate to buy it if under pressure to do so. By the way, I used that truck for over a year and then sold it for $850.00 more than I paid for it.

Now back to the exponential profit subject at hand. After I had finished about half of my first cup of coffee, I came across the following classified ad:

"14ft alum. Grumman canoe, w/Minnkota trolling motor, 2 seat cushions, 2 life preservers, NO leaks. Good cond. $300 for all..."

My thoughts then went back to my objective of doubling my $260.00. I immediately turned on my trusty ole computer and began to research the values of a Grumman canoe and a Minnkota trolling motor. There were many years, models, and sizes of both, but I concluded that if I could buy all of the man's stuff with my $260.00, I should able to sell the boat and the motor separately for enough to again double my investment.

I called and inquired as to where I could see the items. The gentleman gave me his address and I began my journey on another great hunt. When I arrived at the address, there was stuff all over the place. The lawn was lined with appliances, mowers, tools, and many other items of unknown origin or purpose. I thought to myself, "Look here, look here, you have hit the mother load." The first thing that I wanted to know was why he was selling all his stuff. Now this point is very important why buying stuff; unless the seller has a good reason to sell, I know that I am not likely to get a good deal as a buyer. I will expand on this subject later on when I tell you about my five "D's," but for now, just know that the subject is important. The seller told me that he had "found the Lord," and that he was being "dislocated" to another country to do charity work for "Him." Now if this isn't a good reason to get rid of your stuff, I don't know what is. It is my policy to try to never offer any more than about 75% to 90% of the maximum that I am willing to pay, unless of course, there are other buyers waiting and I am already looking at a good deal. Offering no more than the 75% to 90% leaves some room in case you happen upon a seller who too likes to negotiate. Also, you never know when a seller will take you up on your offer.

Before going to see the items, I had already calculated that 75% of my $260.00 was approximately $200.00. I checked out the canoe and the trolling motor. Realizing that both were in top-notch condition, I proceeded to tell the seller that the items could very well be worth what he was asking, but that I had only $200.00 that I wanted to spend on a boat and motor. Meanwhile, I noticed a nice looking clothes dryer sitting next to the boat, so I thought what the heck, I'm going to now find out how bad he wants to unload his stuff in order for him to be able to move on with his "calling." So, I continued by telling him that I would give him my $200.00 cash, right then, for the boat and the motor, if, he would throw in the dryer. Much to my surprise, he immediately said, "I can't take this stuff with me, so I will take it." I could not help but wonder what else I could have gotten with my $200.00 if I had tried harder. I paid him the $200.00 and noticed that he also had a nice looking riding mower parked in his front yard with a "for sale" sign on it. It was only 3 or 4 months old and was just like new. It was an approximately $1,500.00 mower that he had priced at $800.00. To make a long story short, I bought it for $600.00 and later sold my old Craftsman mower, which I had used for 16 years, for my asking price of $425.00. I now had a new riding mower with only $175.00 more invested. This mower story doesn't have much to do with my business investments, but I thought that you might find it interesting since it was associated with the boat and motor transaction. I always try to maintain an awareness of unexpected items for sale; and, go prepared to negotiate for their purchase if I can immediately see a profit in the deal. I was then the proud owner of a canoe, a trolling motor, 2 boat paddles, 2 cushions, and a couple of life preservers; and oh yes, don't forget the clothes dryer and lawn mower. I will let your imagination paint your mind a picture of Betty's face when I came home with all that "junk." She obviously did not share the pleasure that I received from the results of my hunt in the wild.

As planned before the culmination of my high-level business deal, I drafted three classified advertisements for the resale of my stuff, as follows:

"CANOE – alum, 14', 2 paddles, 2 life jackets, 2 cushions. Exc. cond. $385..."

"TROLLING motor – Minnkota, model 35 4speed. 17lb thrust. $85..."

"DRYER, gas. Excellent condition without a scratch. $150..."

As soon as the ads were published, our phone began ringing. I received at least a dozen calls the first day. Within three days, I had sold all the advertised items. The first couple that came to see the canoe bought it. They were the negotiating type and offered $300.00 for it. I said, "You know, this is really a good canoe and I believe that it is really worth the asking price of $385.00, but, I would be willing to throw in the two life jackets, the two cushions and the paddles for $375.00." The gentleman slowly looked everything over again and said, "Tell you what I will do; I'll give you $325.00." The lady seemed to be less of a negotiator than her husband, so I looked at her and said that surely all of it was worth at least $350.00. The lady then said that they had some grandchildren coming to visit them and that she really would like to have the canoe for them to use while they were here. I just kept quiet, and after what seemed like a long time, the gentleman said, "I guess we'll take it." I told him that he sure was a good negotiator and that they are getting a real good deal. I got the impression that he was more concerned about his wife's impression of him as a negotiator than he was for the price that he was paying. I always do my best to permit the buyer to leave the deal with the feeling that he came out a winner. The lady paid me the $350.00 and they left as the proud owners of a canoe tied down to the top of their car.

Needless to say, I would have been happy with their first offer of $300.00, especially considering that I had paid only $200.00 for everything. However, had I told them that I would not take their offer of $300.00, I would have lost my negotiating power to return to that price in order to make the sale if I needed to do so. There is a lesson in this story that you might want to make note of; and that is, I am always cautious about refusing an offer unless I really mean it.

Instead, I emphasize that I believe the item to be worth more than the offer and continue to negotiate until I reach a win-win situation.

The trolling motor was probably the easiest of all the items to sell. A gentleman called and said that if it was in good condition, that he would take it. He arrived about 10 minutes early for his appointment, looked the motor over, and paid me my asking price of $85.00. He obviously was of the non-negotiating type.

The clothes dryer, which really was in good condition, was the last item to sell. A lady called and told me that she had been looking for one like mine for a long time. She said that there were lots of used electric dryers for sale, but that she had wanted to buy a gas dryer, which this one was. She told me that she had the cash to buy it with and asked me if I would hold it for her until she could come to get it. I told her that I really needed to sell it to the first person that came to buy it. She then told me that she would come to see it within the next 30 minutes. She showed up as planned, bought the dryer, and paid me the $150.00 asking price in cash. I always try to make the sale while the buyer is in the notion to buy. I never "hold" an item for anyone, because if I do, I cannot sell it to a real buyer when they come along. Also, it seems that every time that I have "held" something for someone, I never did hear from them again.

Let us get our breath for a minute and analyze where I was at that time in relation to my plan to maintaining the exponential growth of my investment. I began this adventure with $260.00 and sold all three items for a total of $585.00. Not only did I double my investment, I made an additional $65.00, which equaled a 125 percent profit. I thought to myself, "mission accomplished," as I mowed my lawn riding high in the saddle of my new shiny mower. I'll bet my neighbors where thinking, "How in the world does that man afford all the new stuff that he buys? I'll bet that we make more money than he does!" We will just let the answer to that question be our secret won't we?

I never again heard from the gentleman from whom I purchased all the stuff. I'll bet that he is in some third world country with a lot of little big-eyed children hanging off his shirttail. I'll also bet that he is at least fifty pounds lighter than he was when I met him because at that time, he sure was a big ole boy. Wherever he is, I honestly do hope that he is well, serving a good purpose and has re-assembled any "stuff" that he might need.

CHAPTER FIVE

The Temptation of a Tempo

I was raised in Winston, Kentucky, a great little rural community located in the foothills of the Appalachian Mountains. The adjoining county to the west of ours was considered to be in the "Bluegrass Region" of Kentucky, a land of rich soil that produces an abundance of high quality tobacco, corn, cattle, fast race horses, and pretty women; or is it pretty horses and fast women? Anyway, in my home county, most businesses are in some way dependent upon the timber and coal industries.   Perhaps the only thing that the two counties have in common is their separation by a little creek; called "Turpin Creek" by the way, but that is yet another story for another time. As an adolescent, I rarely crossed that creek because I was taught to believe that the fine residents of that other county were "uppity-uppity" and thought that they were "too good for us." Now I'm not going to try to define "uppity-uppity" because my word processor did not indicate that it was a misspelled word, therefore, it must be rather common and you more than likely know what it means.

I got my first car when I was sixteen. After giving it a good wash job and a couple coats of wax, I decided to fill it up with gas and venture across that social-dividing creek and investigate the quantity and quality of the opposite sex that surely must be plentiful in that grassy flatland of "milk and honey." A good friend of mine once told another friend, and in my presence, "You know, ole 'Turp' here was raised up there in them mountains and it took him sixteen years to get up enough nerve to cross the creek and come over here to our county. But here he came, one tree at a time. He would look around a tree, see his way clear to the next, and run like hell before something got him. Now, he's got the prettiest wife in the county and owns half the town." Owning half the town was a gross overstatement, however, I did own my share of it. But my friend was absolutely right when he said that I had the prettiest wife in town; and I still do by the way.

A problem that I have always had is keeping Betty, my wife. Other men have always wanted her so I have had to stay on my toes all these years to keep one from snatching her up and running off with her. My point here is that this is what happens when you have something nice that other people want. But on the other hand, and after giving this some more thought, maybe she is still with me because she can't get rid of me. Either way, there is one thing that I have learned for sure, if you have something that other people want, the last thing in the world that you need to worry about is whether or not you are a "salesman."

Many authors have written books on the subject of the "art of selling." I believe that the tactics they describe apply to the efforts of someone trying to sell something that no one wants. If you have something for sale that other people want, it will sell itself; all you will need to do is let others know that you have it for sale. If you buy stuff for resale that no one wants, you will be lucky to sell it for any profit, no matter how good a salesman you might be.

Over and over again, people tell me that they could never buy and sell stuff for a profit because, as they say, "I'm just not a salesman." Now think about this for a moment; what picture does your mind conjure up when you hear the word "salesman?" More than likely you would describe the person as being "slick," lacking in honesty, high pressure, a flipper of spandex-waist paints, wearer of an old tie with gravy stains on it and loose at the neck, and in your face trying to sell you something that is of poor quality that you don't want in the first place. If this is the picture that you have of a salesman, then I don't blame you for not wanting to be one, much less claiming that you are one. I'm telling you to forget about trying to be a salesman because it is absolutely a mute point in the game of making money. In others words, don't try to be a salesperson, instead, simply be a person with something of quality for sale. If there is any art in selling, it surely must be in the art of buying stuff that people want. Therefore, I am convinced, beyond any doubt, that you make your money when you buy, not when you sell. You must buy high quality at below market value. Therefore, the art of negotiating, not selling, is a matter of great importance. The "do's" and "don'ts" of this art have been incorporated throughout the transactions described in this book.

All this talk about stuff that other people want leads me to the next exponential growth deal that I made. It will clearly demonstrate the importance of dealing in quality stuff and being honest in all representations. With the $585.00 that I had earned now in my pocket, I again started my search for something else to buy that I could resell at a 100% profit. The classified ad read:

"85 FORD TEMPO, 64K miles, very good condition, $700/obo..."

My first impression was that any 1985 car with only 64,000 miles on it should be in good condition. I also thought that perhaps I could buy it for $600.00 since the ad said obo (or best offer), and if so, I could throw in the extra $15.00 that would be needed to make the deal. My next step was to research the car's value in order to get an idea as to whether or not I could resell it for a much as $1,200.00. Once again I cranked up my computer and searched the various websites for values. I learned that it was worth $1,150.00 wholesale and $1,500.00 average retail. Also, $55.00 could be added to both values as a low mileage factor. It was obvious that the price of the car was a good deal and that I could probably double my investment even if the seller would take no less than the asking price.

I made the call early that morning and arranged to see it within 30 minutes. I also learned from the call that the lady was selling the car, which was hers, because her husband was ill and they were moving back up north in order to be near his family. She said that she had inherited the car from her aunt and no

51

longer need it. I concluded that the car must have been driven by two adult females and that it probably really was a nice car.

When I arrived, the Tempo was parked at the curb next to the street. I could tell from a distance that it was obviously in very good condition. By the way, I have learned that in most cases your first impression of an item is probably correct. I introduced myself and began an inspection of the vehicle. It was obviously in original condition without any new paint jobs or major repairs having been performed or now needed. I asked if she knew of anything at all that might be wrong with the car. She looked me straight in the eye and told me that it was in perfect condition, but that she just didn't need it anymore.

I noticed that the air conditioning system did not blow air as cold as it should. It appeared to only need a simple recharge of refrigerant. The seats, dash, headliner, carpets, and rest of the interior were in outstanding condition and very clean. Also, the trunk was clean and the carpet looked like new. All four tires were good and the spare apparently had never been used. After a short drive around the block in it, I concluded that it was the best 1985 automobile that anyone could find in a long time.

I told the lady that I was interested in the car but that I was very concerned about the air conditioning. I told her that in most cases, it would cost from $1,000.00 to $2,000.00 to replace the system; which was true by the way. I also told her that it could be that all it needed was a recharge, which of course would not cost near that much. All of that was said to create some doubt in the seller's mind about the value of the car. After some hesitation and displaying a look of deep concern, I asked her if she would be willing, under the circumstances, to take $600.00 cash for it right then. She said, after only a slight hesitation, "I really need to sell it so I'm going to let you have it."

She went into her house to get the title. Meanwhile, I counted out $600.00 cash to pay for the car, using my $585.00 plus $15.00 "out of pocket." When she returned, I checked the title to verify that there were no liens against the car and that the vehicle identification number, known as the "VIN," matched that of the vehicle. When dealing in vehicles, I always double check the VIN number to make sure that I am not buying a stolen vehicle. I also ensure that the seller is the legal owner with the legal right the sell the vehicle, and that all the listed owners sign the title with their name exactly as it appears in the official printed section of the title. In this case, she was the sole owner and her signature was in fact as it appeared on the title. I paid her for the car and told her that I would be back to pick it up within an hour.

When I got the car home, I decided to see if I could recharge the air conditioning system myself. Using one of the simple and inexpensive connection tools and a small can of refrigerant, I was able to get the system "blowing cold as ice" within only a few minutes. I checked it again the next day and it was obvious that the minor problem had been solved. The car was in such a good condition that there was nothing else to do to it.

I had used one of the major online services to sell a few other items in the past and decided to use it again to sell my Tempo. My history of business on the site provided me with a perfect rating with the firm. I could therefore use the

53

"Buy It Now" method of selling. In other words, I could list the car on the auction portion of the site, with a reserve bid, and also provide a buyer with the opportunity to buy it immediately at a set price. I set my "But It Now" price at $1,475.00, which was $25.00 under the average retail value. I concluded that if there was anyone out there looking an outstanding used car in the $1,500.00 range, it would be difficult for them to not check out my Tempo. Also, keep in mind that if I could sell the car for $1,475.00, I would make $875.00 profit, or approximately 146 percent return on my investment.

In the ad, I included a picture of the exterior, one of the front interior and one of the rear seat a floor. The ad read:

"Ford Tempo GL 4-door sedan, very low miles, senior owned and driven. 64,855 miles, automatic transmission, economical 4 cylinder gas engine, air conditioning, cruise control, and silver in color"

The first day that the car was advertised, I received an email from a gentleman who requested some additional pictures of the car. He said that he was looking for an inexpensive and reliable car for his recently divorced daughter. He asked if I would personally trust the car enough for my own daughter and 2-year-old grandson to ride around town in it. He said that he was ready to use the "Buy It Now" option if he was convinced that the car was in good and safe condition. Having inspected the car thoroughly before buying it, and again after getting it home, I could comfortably and honestly answer "Yes" to his question about its reliability and safety. This is an example of what I mean when I say that you must deal only in quality stuff and avoid so-called bargains.

By then, I had already received 7 bids on the car, but none of them had reached the $1,375.00 reserve price that I had established for the auction. The next morning I took some additional pictures of the car and emailed them to the gentleman who was interested in it for his daughter. In my email to him, I said:

"Thanks for your inquiry. In response to your question, the answer is YES! I would be perfectly happy to have my daughter and 2-year-old grandson, if I had a daughter and a grandson, drive the car around town. The pictures that you requested are attached. As they say, 'pictures are worth a thousand words.' As you will see, the interior and trunk of this car are as clean as most 2000 models that you will find today. Let me know if you have any additional questions. For your information, I have already had 7 bids on it the first day."

Such a subtle hint about the possibility of a fast sale is always a good practice. When a prospective buyer is really interested in the item that you have for sale, he or she will always be concerned about it being sold to someone else if they personally don't buy it real soon. I truly believe that informing the gentleman about already receiving 7 bids on the car was definitely a contributing factor to his decision to use the "Buy It Now" option.

The buyer's next email to me stated:

"Your pictures WERE worth a thousand words. Daughter wants the car. We will take it, just did the Buy It Now option on the car. Send me directions to your place and we will come down on Sunday with cash, or, whatever payment type you prefer. Thank you for the additional photos…"

I then checked my email and sure enough, I had a message from the auction site informing me that the item had been sold. I am always amazed by the speed and convenience of modern technology. I can't help but wonder how the history of Texas would be different had Davy Crocket and Daniel Boone had laptop computers to use for communicating with the world outside the Alamo.

One of the greatest satisfactions that I receive out of a consummated deal, in addition to the profit of course, is the knowledge that the buyer is satisfied with the item. Having a high quality item for sale and having been honest with the buyer resulted in me receiving the following unsolicited email a few days later:

"You were more than right – it is the best $1500 car in the country – I could have looked for another six months and never seen one as good as this – drove straight back to Jacksonville, one stop at the rest stop on I-10, not a hiccup, burp, or wobble out of the car…nearly perfect on all counts. I feel very comfortable with my daughter and grandson being in this car. It was worth the drive!! Thank you!! My daughter is thrilled with it!"

I then sent him a message acknowledging his email and thanked him for his compliments. I also told him that honesty and integrity were very important in such matters. Seventeen days later, I received the following unexpected email message from him:

"Just wanted to thank you again about the car. My mechanic was very impressed with the condition of the car for an 85. I had him go through the entire car just to make sure there was nothing wrong anywhere and look for potential problems."

I am still very pleased with the outcome of this deal on the 1985 Ford Tempo and equally happy that my retirement gift of $100.00 had grown to $1,475.00. I would like to again remind you that the final transaction was the result of a person having something of quality for sale rather than that person being a salesman. Perhaps you still don't believe that you can become a salesman, and it is ok if you don't, but I do hope you are now convinced that you too can become a person with something good for sale that other people want. Give it a try and I believe that you will be happy with and proud of the results.

CHAPTER SIX

Leverage for a Motorcycle

After selling the Ford Tempo, my $100 gift had grown to $1,475.00; how about them apples? Up until then, it had been fairly easy to find stuff that I could buy and resale for at least twice my investment. I then realized that finding something for $1,475.00 that I could resell for $2,950.00 was not a reasonable expectation. I'll bet that you too have already thought about that. I believed that I was pretty good at what I was doing, but not that good. Therefore, I concluded that I must apply another tactic if I was going to maintain my exponential growth. I could have purchased two items of "stuff" and continued the financial success that I was then enjoying; but, that would have meant that I must double all my efforts. It would have taken twice the required time to find, buy, advertise, show, and sell in order to continue with my plan. Instead, I decided to continue dealing with only one item at a time as long as possible. I also knew that the value of the single deal items must increase in proportion to the amount that I had to invest if I was to continue the rate of exponential growth.

Most definitions of leverage include such words as "mechanical," "lever" and "power." I believe that such definitions should be expanded to include some additional words such as "business," "money" and "profits." I assure you that the application of leverage in a business deal can be very profitable. I had witnessed a lot of people make a lot of money using other people's money; in other words, operating on borrowed money. I like to think of other people's money as being a tool, like a lever that is rented to use for a short period of time, and definitely not for long periods of time. Therefore, the "rent," known as "interest," becomes a very insignificant and inexpensive cost of doing business, regardless of the percentage rate of interest, as long as it is reasonable of course. I am rarely concerned about the interest rate on a loan because I intend to repay it before such costs become a factor for concern. I decided that I could do the same by using the money that I had received from the sale of the Tempo as leverage, and then borrow enough additional funds to purchase something that I could easily resell for a $1,475.00 profit; which would again double my investment. I concluded that if my $1,475.00 represented a typical down payment of 20%, I should easily be able to borrow enough money to provide me with about $7,500.00 in purchasing power. It was logical to assume that I could find a high quality item priced at that amount, negotiate to buy it for about 10% less and then resell it for about 10% above the $7,500.00. I knew that if I could pull this off, I could once again double my investment and maintain my profit pattern of exponential growth. Please know that the use of leverage in business is certainly not a brainchild of mine. It has been commonly used for a long, long time. My purpose here is to make you more aware of its use and to tell you how I used it to my advantage.

When going to inspect an item, I always go prepared to buy it on the spot. I have learned that the best way to be prepared is to obtain a commitment from my banker, or from whomever I am borrowing money, ahead of time. I tell my lender exactly what I plan to do with the money and the amount that I want to borrow. Here again, honesty is the rule to live by. My motto is that I will negotiate with you until I am blue in the face, but there is no way that I would steal even a penny from you. If at all possible, I go ahead and borrow the maximum amount that I anticipate needing. Another way is to get a letter of credit and use the previous profits as a deposit with the seller. Or, perhaps you can obtain a home equity loan and have ready cash as you need it. As a matter of fact, there are lots and lots of creative financing possibilities, but I don't believe that this is the place or time to discuss that subject in more detail. The method to use depends largely on one's personal financial situation at the time.

The next day after closing the deal on the Tempo, the morning newspaper sported several new classified ads, one of which read:

"01 HARLEY Sportster 1200, low mi, exc. cond., lots of chrome, many extras. $7,500.00..."

The bike was in my price range and it seemed to be priced below market value. Then, as always, I fed the information into my computer and learned that the average retail value of such a bike in my area was between $9,205.00 and $9,710.00. The high value convinced me that the seller was desperate to sell and that I could easily negotiate for an even lower price if I really tried. Needless to say, I knew that I must act fast before someone else bought the bike. That morning, I arranged for a short term small business loan in the amount of $5,525.00 at 6% simple interest. The loan amount, along with my $1,475.00, gave me a total of $7,000.00. I try to never take more money with than I am willing to pay for the item. This will not only prevent me from paying too much, it will encourage me to negotiate for an even lower price. Yea, I know, what will happen if the seller won't take less than the asking price? The answer is simple, I won't buy the item. But I will also tell you that I have never had a problem with, or lost money on, something that I didn't buy. Now think about that for a moment. The world is full of stuff to buy and sell, so why be concerned about not buying something on which you cannot make a good profit?

It was about 9:15 am when I placed the call. I really do believe that I got the gentleman out of bed, because at first, he sounded like he had a mouth full of caramel candy or something stickier. It was about a 35 minute drive across town to his house but I made it in 30. He raised the garage door and I didn't see a motorcycle anywhere. He then walked over to the corner of the garage and started removing a blanket from what appeared to be several pieces of furniture. Low and behold, there amongst several other items of unknown purposes, sat the Harley Davidson shining like new. I checked to make sure that there was no oil on the floor, which if there was, would be a good indication that the bike

61

leaked oil. Everything was clean and there was no sign of repairs having been performed on the bike.

After he backed the motorcycle out of the garage, he turned on the gas and started it. It easily started and ran great. I then asked if he had any accessories that went with it, such as helmets. Now take note of the timing of this question and the fact that we had not yet begun negotiations on price. If price has not been discussed, a seller will normally include anything in the deal that he can to entice a buyer to buy. If an agreement has been made on price, you normally will not be able to negotiate for any additional items, terms or conditions. This is true whether the deal is worth ten dollars or ten million dollars. The seller then told me that he would throw in a helmet, a lock, leather tool bag, some oil, and a kit to be used for cleaning the air filter. I asked him if he would be willing to ride the bike to my home for me, providing that we could come to an agreement on the price. He said that he would be happy to do that. I then asked him a very important question and watched his body language as he answered it. I asked him if he knew of anything whatsoever that was wrong with the bike. Without any hesitation, he said, "Absolutely not." Always ask the seller if he knows of any problems with the item, and then wait for his response. If he is being honest, he will look you straight in the eye when answering. Normally, you will get an honest answer; that is, if you have not yet agreed on a price.

Now came the negotiating part of the transaction. I always ask the question, "Why are you selling it?" The answer will most likely provide you with an indication of whether or not the seller is willing to negotiate. With a good reason to sell, the seller might sell you the item for much less that you dreamed possible. Besides, how can you know for sure if you don't try? I am always disappointed when a seller takes me up on my first offer because that convinces me that I did not do the best job of negotiating for a lower price. He told me that he was "Out of work," living with his parents and really needed the money.

I then confirmed the asking price by saying, "Was it $7,500.00 that you are asking for it?" He said, "Yes, and I know it is worth every penny of it." I then quickly said, "Oh, I'm not questioning its value; it could very well be worth what you are asking for it, or maybe even more." Important point here; never, ever ask the seller for the least amount that he will take for something, or say, "What is your bottom dollar?" If you do, you will eliminate any possibility of further negotiations because the seller will "lose face" if he goes below the price that he quotes to you. I continued by saying, "You might be able to get your asking price if you are willing to hold out for it long enough, and, perhaps help a possible buyer come up with the financing to buy it." I then told him that I was just hoping to buy the bike for quite a bit less because of the limited funds that I had available to spend on a motorcycle. He then said, "I was hoping to get at least $7,000.00 out of it." Now when a seller voluntarily comes off his asking price by such a large percentage and in that manner, you can rest assured that in most cases he will negotiate for an even lower price. I took my time looking the bike over again, and with a slight frown and hesitation, I said, "Tell you what I am able to do; I can come up with $6,800.00 cash to take the bike off your hands right now; and again, I'm not saying that it isn't worth $7,000.00, I'm only saying that this is all that I am in a position to spend right now." I was determined to not say another word until he gave me his answer. After turning, twisting and wrestling with a decision for some time, he said, "I hate to, but I'm going to trade with you." Bingo! I was successful in negotiating $700.00 off the asking price, even thought it was an excellent price to begin with. I have said it before and will probably say it many times again; you make your money when you buy, not when you sell. Remember what I said before; a desirable item at a fair price will sell itself. It therefore stands to reason that you should concentrate your efforts on buying rather than the "art of selling," as some people call it.

I have learned, the hard way in some cases, that the importance of knowing the resaleability of whatever it is that I am buying is extremely important. (My spell checker just informed me that there is no such word as "resaleability." So what, there is now. I'm sure that you know what it means so I will continue to use it.) There are several factors that influence resaleability. For example, year, make, model, color, mileage, size, condition, etc; and yes, believe it or not, even smell. I would not buy a used car one time because apparently the seller's cats had used the back seat as a litter box and the odor was awful.

It is always advisable to be an expert in whatever it is that you are buying or selling. Among other things, being an expert simply means knowing what is popular. If you buy something that no one wants, I assure you that you will not make any money because you cannot resell if for a profit. As a matter of fact, you might even have to sell it at a loss in order to move on.

I would like to share with you some facts on this subject that I have learned somewhere along the way. Perhaps they will help you to become a better expert in your area of interest. Buying something for resale can be a risky business activity if you let your personal biases and opinions influence your decisions on what to buy. I believe that this is known as, what some people would call, a subjective decision. On the other hand, most of the risk can be eliminated, as well as making the process a lot easier, by applying the objective approach. That is, buy that which is most popular in each of the areas of concern and then there will be no need for you to take your brain to task for an opinion.

Let's use the Harley deal to briefly expand on the factors that influence resaleability. The year of the bike was a 2001. During the current year, I try to buy something for resell that was built (or made, put together or whatever) less than 5 years prior. Also, I have noticed that people seem to have a mental block of some kind that prevents them from buying a 1999 anything if they can possibly buy a 2000 or later model. I suggest that it is because they don't want to tell their friends that the thing, whatever it might be, is a 1999 because that sounds as if it is old; whereas a 2000 sounds as if it is almost new. I did a little research on this subject using my trusty NADA Value Guide. I was curious about the comparison of drops in the percentages of values between the same vehicle from 2001 down to 2000, from 2000 down to a 1999 and then 1999 down to 1998. I used the value of a motor home for this little project. Here is the bottom line; the percentage of decrease in value from a 2000 to a 1999 was double that of the other years. Now I know that my friend Paul, a university professor who teaches research, would probably tell me that this is not true research. I'm sure that it isn't, however, it is close enough to convince me to buy something for resale that is a 2000 or newer.

There is another side to this year matter that I also noticed. Let's say for example that the Harley was a 2003. The NADA average retail of that year of the same bike is $10,150.00. I want to ask you a question here; why would anyone buy such a bike from me when they can make a little trip up to their local Harley Davidson dealer a buy a new one for only a few more dollars? I'm sure that you have heard about the largest amount of depreciation occurring on a vehicle during the first year. I have too and agree that this is true. However, it seems that people are willing to take that loss for three reasons: first, they hold the bragging rites to a new vehicle; secondly, they like the secure feeling of a one-year manufacturer's warranty that is usually included; and thirdly, it is usually easier to obtain financing on a new vehicle as opposed to a used one. I have therefore concluded that when dealing in vehicles, I need to buy one that is between two and four years old if I am going to resell it in the least amount of time and for the most profit.

I never let my temptation to buy a bargain override the necessity of buying a good brand of anything to resell. Also, I never let my personal preferences override the necessity of buying a brand that is most popular. For example, it might be that you really do like the brand of a motorcycle that is made in some small third world country because it has bull horns on the front, a whip antenna on the back, whitewall tires, mud flaps, and a noise maker in the spokes. If you only paid $87.00 for such a monster, you really got a bargain but I assure you that when it comes time to resell it, you will be sorry that it isn't a popular brand at a good deal rather than a bargain. Personally, I avoid bargains, I only consider good deals. Now I need to say something here; I do not have any stock in the Harley Davidson Motorcycle Company, nor do I want any because I want to personally be in control of my money at all times. I'm just using the motorcycle as an example of the importance of buying with the objective of reselling in mind.

Next, how about the matter of model? Here again the rule is simple; just buy the most popular one, whatever it is that you are buying to resell. When I'm talking about model, I don't mean the year of the vehicle. As an example, the model identifies it is as being a station wagon or a pickup truck. Check out the highways and compare the number of station wagons you see in relation to the number of pickup trucks. Get my drift? Which would you buy to resell, a station wagon or a pickup? The answer to that question is simple; however, I believe that it serves to help illustrate my point. The motorcycle in this case was an XL 1200 cc Sportster. Now Harley also builds an 883 cc Sportster, but I believe that people who ride Harleys want the most power that they can get for the size. I personally always buy the most popular model of anything for my personal use as long as it is in my price range; and I'll bet that you do too.

Also, I know to not overlook the importance of color. A 2000 Chevrolet pickup truck with only 35,000 miles on it would certainly be a good item to buy for resale; that is, if you can negotiate for a good deal. But now let me ask you this; would you buy it if it is pink? Probably not, that is if you are in your right mind, because

67

you would have one heck of a time reselling it, although all the other factors are favorable. See what I mean about the importance of color? How many pink pickups do you see on the road? What good-ole-boy with a pinch of snuff under his lip would buy a pink pickup? Pay a few dollars more and get a red one, or perhaps white or blue but be sure to pass on the pink one. In the case of my motorcycle, it was a popular color very similar to the new models.

Low mileage on a vehicle can easily override another factor which might be undesirable. The Harley that I bought only had 6,000 miles on it. This would be quite a few for a 2003 for example, but it is considerably low for a 2001. Remember the old Ford Tempo with 64,855 miles that I bought and sold? That was a case in which the old year was overridden by the desirable make, model, color, size, and especially, the condition. It is a fact that there are a lot of people out there that cannot afford a car costing over $1,500.00.

I could go on and on with stories about size, condition etc, but in summary of the subject of resaleability, I have learned that popularity, popularity and popularity are the three most important factors to consider in the matters of year, make, model, color, mileage, size, condition, etc. of whatever it is that I buy to resell. I realize that this is a simple approach to becoming an expert, but believe me, it works.

Since the Ford Tempo sold in only a couple of days, I decided to try selling the Harley online. My ad read, "2001 Harley-Davidson Sportster XL 1200 with only 5,982 miles, like new." A couple of other subjects of importance had to be addressed; terms of the sale and shipment of the item. I knew that I was not going to accept a personal check from anyone, and, that I was not about to ship a motorcycle anywhere. Therefore, I noted in the ad that I would accept only cash or cashier's check as payment at the time of picking up the motorcycle at my address; no shipping. I further stated in the ad that any and all required sales tax and other government required fees were to be paid by the buyer. I always provide details on all major terms and conditions in an ad because I don't want to get stuck with any associated fees or other costs.

Investing in a good digital camera is wise because pictures are very valuable in an ad. I took about a dozen pictures of the Harley and selected four for my ad. I always like to study my pictures very carefully to ensure that they are of good quality, show the item at its best, and that there are no items in the picture that will distract from the intended purpose of creating a desire to own. For example, I eliminated some of the pictures because the angle of the light caused a portion of the bike to appear flawed or damaged. A professional photographer I am not, but I do try to select pictures with a background that highlights the best features of the item that I have for sale.

The ad was posted online the same day that I purchased the bike and it ran for seven days. By the way, I have a policy that I do not buy anything that I cannot, for whatever the reason, place back on the market the following day or shortly thereafter; because the faster that I can turn deals, the more money I will make. Buying something to "fix up" to resell for a profit is not in my realm of interests.

During the next seven days, I checked my email for any inquiries and for the results of the auction. My excitement about this project began to dwindle as the days went by without any positive results. We all know that there a lot of shysters in this world, and if you think for a moment that they will not target you, you are dead wrong. They will, and they did; and I was their target. The only response that I received from that first ad was from someone claiming the name of "Danny" from Antwerp Belgium; that's right, Belgium. After reading his email, I knew that I was a target for an obvious scam. He said:

"Complements of the day. Hope you had a splendid Easter celebration. I am Danny by name, a bike/car dealer based in Antwerp Belgium. I recently saw your advert as regards the bike you want to sell. The high demand of your type of bike both for the local and international market has made it imperative that we should go into this transaction with a view to fostering a harmonious business relationship that will stand the taste of time. In the past, I have concentrated my business in the European market, but recently came to understand that one could get cheaper and better bikes from the US market. Based on this, I will like us to treat this transaction with the seriousness it deserves. Hope the bike is in perfect mechanical and cosmetic condition. I will like to have an in-depth description of the present condition of the bike. Get back to me ASAP."

Now let me ask you, have you ever heard such bull in your life? In most cases like this, the scam artist will notify you that someone near you owes him money in an amount that is about double the price of the item that you are selling and that he will just have him bring the check by to you rather than sending it to him. All he asks is that you send him a certified check for the difference. Surprise, surprise; if you fall for a scam like this by accepting such a check, you will soon learn that it is colder than a sunbather's butt on the North Pole. I simply ignored that email that I had received.

I received one other response from this first online ad. Some gentleman in Erie, Pennsylvania informed me by email that I was asking too much for the bike because he could buy a new one up there for my "buy-now" price. However, he would be willing to drive to Florida to buy mine for $7,000.00. Now have you ever heard of such foolishness? My response to him was, "If you can buy a new one in Erie for my price, why are you bothering to contact me?" I never heard from him again.

My flow of previous good luck on fast sales had obviously dwindled to a trickle, but I decided to give the online possibility another chance, using the same type ad and advertising at same price. Not much changed during the next seven days. The only response that I received was an email from another con artist in some other country. The inquiry asked for the least that I would take for the bike. I responded with a price that would provide me with a profit equal to double my investment. The next email that I received from the character said:

"Thanks for the mail, am okay with the price so how are you doing about the shipping because I have a reputable who cater on my behalf through out the whole world so what is going to happen is this am going to instruct my client in US who had been owing me the sum of ($15,000.00 US) to issue out the

71

cheque to you so what you going is that immediately the cheque gets to you, you have to deduct your cost price of the 1200CC SPORTST2001 HARLEY DAVIDSON and sent me cashier's cheque for difference."

I responded with the following message:

"If you think that I am going to fall for this bull, then you are full of bull."

I never received another word from that crook.

Two weeks had now passed and I had not received a single serious inquiry from a buyer. I reminded myself that I had for sale a late model, low mileage, popular color, brand name motorcycle at a fair price. The only issue was the fact that a buyer had not yet seen the ad. By now, you probably know that I am not a big hunter or sports fan, but, I do occasionally enjoy fishing. Maybe it is because fishing and business are in many respects a lot alike. People that catch a lot of fish go fishing a lot. They know that you must keep your hook baited and in the water. Then catching fish is just a simple matter of waiting, waiting until the right fish for the bait comes along. You are probably thinking, "How simple!" The point that I am trying to make here is that I have learned to not get disappointed if something doesn't sell as fast as I would like. It will sell; it is just a matter of time. When I was in the real estate business, I had some homes that sold within a week and others that I thought would also sell fast take a year to sell; but they did finally sell. As popularity, popularity, and popularity are important when selecting "stuff" to buy for resale, patience, patience, and patience are the three most important personal traits to develop when selling. If you don't, you are likely to sell your stuff too cheap and give up on advancing your cause. A buyer will come along; it is just a matter of time. Constantly reducing the asking price in an attempt to attract a buyer is usually a costly mistake.

With a rather thorough working knowledge of the time factor in selling, I decided to try an approach other than online. I placed a classified ad, under the heading of used motorcycles for sale, in our local newspaper. It read:

"01 HARLEY 1200cc SPORTSTER XL. Always garaged, low miles, like new. Must sell. NADA $9,710. Asking $8,600..."

Two more weeks passed after the ad was published in the newspaper. Including the two weeks that I had advertised online, over a month had passed without a single phone call. I believe that most sellers would start to question their ability to judge at this point. Such a lack of response usually results in a natural tendency to believe that a mistake was made in choosing the item for resale; or, perhaps the price is too high. In reviewing my previous decisions, I again realized that I was selling a desirable item at a reasonable price. I concluded that instead of there being a problem, the lack of response was simply a matter of a buyer not yet seeing the ad; therefore, lowering the asking price would not speed up the process of selling.

On the fifteenth day that the ad ran in the newspaper, I received the call that I had been waiting for. At first, I highly doubted the seriousness or legitimacy of the call. The gentleman asked me for the location where the bike could be seen, and said, "It sounds like just what I have been looking for." That part of the conversation sounded good, but, later on during the call he said that if his friend really liked it, he could pay cash for it on the spot. Our conversation was very

73

confusing because if he wanted a bike like mine, why would a friend of his buy it for cash. I erroneously concluded that this too was some kind of a scam. I learned from the previous attempted scams to be extremely cautious in business dealings, but I also learned from that call to not rule out someone as a buyer until after you get all the facts.

The caller came to see the bike on the afternoon of his inquiry. Based on my suspicions of his intentions, I got out my camera for the purpose of taking a picture of him, along with one of his vehicle and license plate, for use to track him down if I ever needed to do so. However, I learned to treat any prospect as the person who will eventually buy the item. In other words, I am never too hasty in ruling out someone as a buyer based on my initial impression of the person.

When he arrived, I had the motorcycle covered with a clean sheet and parked in my garage. I told him that he was about to see the most perfect 2001 motorcycle that he would ever see in his life. After building up his anticipation, I slowly uncovered the bike. There is just something about such an unveiling that appeals to a buyer, especially if the item is exactly what he or she has been looking for. It also gives the impression that the item has been well cared for.

He looked the bike over and asked if he could hear it run. I gave him the key and he started it. As always, it started easily and ran perfectly. He said that he really liked it but that his friend would need to see it. I was still having a problem with understanding why it was so important that his friend see it. He asked if he could ride the bike to his friend's house. I told him that it was not licensed and that I did not have any insurance on it. Therefore, I couldn't go along with that.

74

He then went around to the front of our home and apparently called his friend on his cell phone. After coming back around the house, he said that it would be a couple of hours before his friend could come by to see it. He then again informed me that if his friend liked the bike, he would pay cash for it on the spot. After hearing this for the second or third time, I could not resist asking him what his friend had to do with the deal. He said that he had put a real estate deal together for his friend and was promised a Harley for his efforts. I asked, "What kind of a real estate deal?" He then proceeded to tell me about how good his friend is at "horse trading" and that he is an excellent negotiator. Now all the events started to make a little sense to me. It sounded to me like he was about to receive some kind of a bribe, but I wasn't about to dig into the matter any deeper. All I was concerned about was the apparent fact that his friend could afford the motorcycle. Knowing that the gentleman in my presence really liked the bike, I did not believe that it made a lot of difference whether his friend liked it or not. I further concluded that he wanted his friend to come by to do the negotiating with me. Realizing this, I knew that I had to be prepared to negotiate and little with the friend in order to make them both feel that their exercise to get a lower price was worth their effort. Also, I assumed that it was important that the friend appear to be the winner of any negotiations. The bottom line was the fact that I would be dealing with a "pinch-hitter" negotiator and therefore had to be prepared to deal with the situation. Before leaving, the gentleman asked if I would take $7,500.00 for the bike. I told him, "absolutely not," and did not counter his offer. He asked if I could give any on the price and I told him that I could probably let him have it for $8,600.00. He then left and said that he would try to get his friend to come by later that day. I frankly never thought that I would ever see him again. That assumption was wrong.

Later that morning, the gentleman called me on my cell phone and told me that he and his friend could meet me at our home in about thirty minutes. When they arrived, I noticed that the one who wanted the bike was a passenger with the man who was apparently his friend. I was then reasonably sure that the bike was sold because it was obvious that his friend was dropping him off in order for him to ride the bike home. Based on that observation, I decided to let the friend negotiate with me to a point no lower than $8,300.00. This would permit me to meet my objective and allow his friend to make a good showing by buying the bike for less that the $8,600.00. The friend looked the bike over and said, "Say you want $8,600.00 for it?" I said, "Yes." He said, "I'll give you $8,000.00 for it." I said, "Can't do it." He then said, "What is the least that you will take?" I said, "We both know that $8,600.00 is a good deal for such a nice bike." The man that would own the bike interrupted the negotiations by saying, "It really is a nice bike." Boy was that a mistake on his part. He was actually helping my cause rather than that of his friend. The friend then said, "Tell you what I'll do; I'll go $8,200.00 cash for it right now."

Having paid $6,800.00 for the bike, this amount would give me a profit of $1,400.00. Now I must say, it was a sure thing and hard to turn down; but I did. Why? Because I knew two things for sure; first, they came to buy the bike, and secondly, they had the money to pay for it. I believed that they would pay more than $8,200.00 for it, but, I also knew that I had to drop the price enough to make the friend appear as the winner of the negotiations. I then said, "Ok, this is my bottom dollar, $8,300.00, take it or leave it because I know that I can get more than that by holding it a few more days." I also quickly added, "But, I need an answer now because I have got to go and don't have time to mess with this deal any more for a measly hundred dollars." My reason to say that was to imply that the friend was "cheap" or perhaps couldn't afford the bike if he still tried to get it for less than $8,300.00. It worked. The friend said, "Fair enough, we'll take it." With that, he went to his truck and returned with the cash. Meanwhile, the man who would own the bike asked if I had a helmet or any other accessories that went with the bike. Although he should have asked that question before the deal was finalized, I gave him the helmet and the owner's manual; but, I kept the Harley-Davidson lock that I got from the previous owner.

The excitement was over and another "game of business" had been won, thanks in part to the power of leverage. I frankly enjoy the game much more than I do the money. My profit from this deal was $1,500.00, which was $25.00 more than my objective to double the $1,475.00 investment. Granted, there were costs for advertising and interest, however, they were minimal and I paid them out-of-pocket in order to keep my exponential growth on track. Armed with my almost $3,000.00, it was once again time to begin another thrilling "hunt" for the next illusive "stuff" to buy for resell.

CHAPTER SEVEN

First to Arrive Gets the Milk

I had just finished a six-week course entitled "How to Write and Publish Your Own Book" at our local community college. I thought that since I was in the process of actually writing a book, perhaps I should learn some of the "dos" and "don'ts" from an expert. Our instructor, Claudine Dervaes, was very good. I especially appreciated the fact that she had a great deal of practical experience in the field. One of the "don'ts" that she emphasized was to never use old clichés such as, "The early bird gets the worm." I would like to use this means and opportunity to demonstrate to her that I was a good student who listened in class. Therefore, I have come up with my own cliché to replace the old one about the early bird; "The first pig to arrive gets the milk." How's that?

This morning, I learned the importance of being the first to arrive. Therefore I thought that today would be a good day to share my feeling of despair with you.

As usual, I was perusing the classifieds in our newspaper when I came across the following two automobiles for sale:

"92 CAMRY LE. Gold edition, loaded. 80k mi. $2500obo.........."

The second ad read, "92 TOYOTA CAMRY LE 4cy, auto, good cond, original owner $1200obo.........."

Both offers to sell appeared to be good deals, so I immediately used the internet to find the values of each. The average retail value of the one listed at $2,500.00 was $4,925.00 and the one listed at $1,200.00 was $4,125.00. If I had bought both of the cars for the total asking prices of $3,700.00, although I'm sure that I could have bought them for a little less, I probably could have sold them for a total of at least $9,050.00. That would have been a profit of $5,350.00 for such a small effort. I had the $3,000.00 from my previous deals and could have easily come up with the other $700.00. Yea, I know, there is the possibility that I would not have made such a handsome profit on the deals. Maybe the cars would not have sold as easily as I believed. Maybe my profit would have only been $4,000.00 instead of $5,350.00. Well whoop-de-do; that still would have permitted me to continue the exponential growth of my previous profits. Yea, I know, this is like being one number off on winning the lottery; which by the way, really happened to me once. However, I still won over $3,000.00 on my ticket.

You are probably wondering how in the world I could let such an exponential profit slip by me so easily. It's simple; I didn't get there in time to get the milk. Someone beat me to it. I later learned that both of the vehicles were in great condition and that both of the sellers had legitimate reasons for selling. When I called about the cars at 9:15 AM, it was too late, they had already been sold. In the past, I have been a little embarrassed to call someone very early in the morning. I have always believed that perhaps the people that I was calling might not yet be awake and that such a call would upset them to the extent that they wouldn't talk to me. Well, you can bet your dialing finger that in the future I will always call about a possible good deal as soon as I find it.   I have learned the hard way that "If you snooze, you loose." (Oops; sorry about that Claudine.)

CHAPTER EIGHT

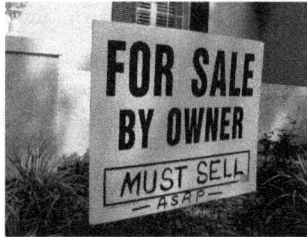

The Six "D" Reasons for Selling

I believe that sellers fall into one of three categories: First, those that are selling for a profit, secondly, those that really want to sell but don't necessarily have to sell, and thirdly, those that have to sell for some reason. The first two categories do not interest me very much because I know that I am not likely to get a good enough deal to accomplish my profit objective. The last category, those that must sell, are the ones that I seek out. Many of these types of sellers will easily negotiate for a low price in order to receive a fast cash sale. For example, I purchased a residential lot in our city from a couple getting a divorce for $5,000.00. Not long before that, they had paid a fair price of $12,500.00 for it. I was a ready, willing and able cash buyer and they wanted to settle their divorce in a hurry and go their separate ways. I later built one of our rental houses on the lot and the investment is still paying off today.

One of the first questions that I try to get answered when considering something to buy for resale is why is the seller selling? The motivating factors for selling that I like to find are related to a divorce, death, debt, disability, displacement, and disposal. I refer to these as my "Six-D's for Selling." I have just given you an example of the divorce "D." The "death "D" is probably my favorite grounds to "farm" for a profitable deal. I especially search out those estates in which the only remaining relatives are siblings, or further removed, who want to sell in a hurry in order to settle their estate. I try to avoid contacting a spouse of the deceased. The best situation is one in which the only survivor is some distant cousin who lives elsewhere. They are usually ready to accept a reasonable and fast cash offer for their property. You might be thinking, "How morbid!" Well if you are, you are not alone. I have been called an "ambulance chaser," plus a few other names that you probably would not repeat from a church pew; but, I buy a lot of property too. This reminds me of the young man who stood on the street corner and requested sexual favors from every attractive female that passed by. A friend of his observed a girl slapping his face and calling him a few choice names. His friend said, "Boy, you must get your face slapped a lot." He answered, "Yea, I do, but I also 'score' a lot." Now back to the important subject at hand, most all of the sellers are grateful for the opportunity to settle their estate in such a fast manner and thank me for my purchase.

You have probably heard about the profits to be made by buying property "on the courthouse steps." Or, perhaps the good deals that people get by buying "repo's" (repossessed property). I'm sure that some people might make some money this way, but debt has not been one of my favorite "D's." In most cases, the owner owes more money on the property that it is worth or they would have sold it to avoid such foreclosures and possibly bankruptcy. And besides, creditors are going to protect their financial interest in the property by buying the property themselves if the bid is much below the market value. Laws are structured to protect lenders; and besides, they did not become lenders by being stupid; at least in most cases this is true. Besides, competition through bidding for such properties usually results in a sale price that is at or near actual retail value. This being the case, I have never been able to see any profit in such a deal. Also, the condition of repossessed property is usually very poor. When the owners know that they are going to lose it to foreclosure, they are not likely to take very good care of it.

Unfortunately, people do become disabled, for various reasons, and can no longer afford the payments on financed properties. They must therefore sell it to avoid foreclosure. This "D" does not frequently happen, in comparison to the other "D's," and therefore is a category in which I prefer to devote little time and effort. But of course, I won't turn down such a deal if it comes along.

The fifth of my six "D's" pertains to potentially good deals resulting from people being geographically dislocated for one reason or another. I know, most people refer to this as being "relocated." However, I prefer "dislocated" because they are being forced to locate in a location different from that which they are presently located; now doesn't that make a lot more since? Perhaps the most common cause of a dislocation is a transfer in employment location. Remember my earlier deal with the canoe, trolling motor, and dryer? That seller was being dislocated by the Lord. He was leaving the country to serve Him and needed to get rid of his stuff in a hurry in order to avoid the wrath of God. Looking back on the situation, maybe the Lord sent me to his rescue. It could very well be that I and I alone prevented him from being dislocated to a place where he would burn forever. Now aren't you proud of me?

The sixth and last "D" results from a seller's desire to dispose of items for one reason or another. A "disposal" sale can result for many reasons, such as retirement for example. Many times the owner of a business is willing to sell items such as vehicles, equipment, tools, machinery, and goods at a reduced price in order to retire. I'm sure that you are familiar with "going-out-of-business" sales. I have learned that the trick to getting a good buy in such situations is to deal directly with the seller before such a sale is implemented. Profitable buying in this type of situation requires a keen sense of what is going on in the business community.

CHAPTER NINE

The Thirty-One Year Old Doublewide

My next project was an old doublewide; a mobile home that was built in 1974. However, it had been fairly well maintained and updated down through the years. I'm happy to report that I not only reached my objective of doubling my investment on this deal, to continue with my planned exponential growth, I tripled it! This was one of my most interesting, profitable and exciting projects.

I called the number in the ad and the lady told me that she could show the home to me at about 2:00 PM the next day. She said that she had several other appointments to show it that same afternoon and would like to make only one trip to the park. I realized that she was using an old selling tactic. Her plan was to put pressure on me to make a commitment to buy the home the first time that I saw it, because if I didn't, one of the many other people coming to see it that afternoon would sign on the dotted line, thereby causing me to "loose out" on the deal. This is an old and perhaps over-used tactic that rarely works.

After a short drive to the mobile home park, I wove my way through the maze of little streets until I found it. There it was; an old mobile home right next to a retention pond. Now if you don't know about Florida retention ponds, let me try to describe one to you. It is a deep man-made depression in the ground ranging in size from a school bus to a football field, built to hold rainwater runoff, during one of our popular storms, instead of having the water flood the surrounding properties. Such ponds are usually enclosed with a chain link fence for the published purpose of protecting children from the dangers of the water. I believe that the real purpose of the fence is to contain alligators; especially when the pond is in an "adult only" park.   Now doesn't this sound logical since old people can't run as fast as children? Others believe that the problem of living next to a retention pond is the presence of mosquitoes the size of superman. If this were a multiple-choice test, I would personally check, "All of the above."

Even though I knew right away that I was not interested in buying the home, I felt obligated to at least show an interest since the owner had taken the time to show it to us. Now you need to know that I was considering a mobile home, as my next project, just after the four back-to-back hurricanes raged through our state. I concluded that any mobile home that could survive such torment couldn't be all bad. However, this one did have several roof shingles missing among other needed parts that made it look like a dog with a bad case of the mange. The interior ceilings showed many signs of leaks that had been amateurishly painted over. Also, the two halves of the home didn't seem to fit together just right. I assumed that the high winds had caused some movements between the parts and pieces. Now that's enough about the one that I didn't buy, let's consider the two-hundred percent profit deal that I did make in that park.

Obviously, the best place to learn more about the park, as well as the other homes that were sale, was the park office. The receptionist was very helpful in providing us with information about the park rules, regulations, amenities, services, and costs. It is a large but well-maintained park of about 500 mobile homes. The lot rent at the time was $359.00 per month and included water, sewer, garbage pickup, mowing, and use of the amenities such as swimming pools, tennis courts, meeting hall, game room, etc. After openly explaining to her that I was only interested in buying for the purpose of reselling for a profit, she quickly informed us of a couple of other homes in the park that were for sale. She volunteered to show them to us while we were there. These two homes, as most of them in the park, were also older ones built in the mid-seventies. One was a partially furnished two-bedroom, two-bath priced at $10,750.00. We were told that the other one was from an estate and that the owners really needed to sell. It was a completely furnished three-bedroom, two-bath home with a separate den and a formal dining room. It also had a nice aluminum carport and a large screened-in porch. It had been improved with vinyl siding and a metal roof. The hurricanes had not damage this home. We were told that the heat and air conditioning system had been checked out and everything worked just fine. Also, that it had been inspected for termites and none were found in the home. The price of this one was $15,000.00. However, she said that it could probably be purchased for a lot less because it had been "sitting" for several months.

Although it needed a little general cleaning, landscape work and routine maintenance, I believed that I could make a reasonable profit on it; if, I could buy it at a price that would permit me to double the $3,000.00 that I had made on my other projects to date. During our visit to the park, I learned that there were several other homes in there for sale, ranging in price from about $7,500.00 to $15,000.00. Therefore, I knew that I would have to buy one at a price that would permit me to add my profit objective of $3,000.00 without exceeding the market for the neighborhood. Now I believe that my professor friend, Paul, would call this logic based on research. Where I'm from, we call it "good horse sense."

I asked the saleslady what she considered to be a fair offer to make on the home. Much to my surprise, she suggested that we make an offer of around $5,000.00 and see what the counter offer would be. Well now let me tell you, this got my attention. There was no doubt in my mind as to whether or not I could make a profit at that purchase price, I just didn't know how much. Although such an offer seemed ridiculously low, considering the condition of the home and that all the personal property was included, I decided to apply my principle of offering at least 10% less no matter what the asking price. So, I made a formal offer of $4,500.00.

After making a confidential phone call, the saleslady returned from her office and said, "We have a deal; they decided to accept your offer." I was very pleased with the news. I had previously decided to apply the business principle of leverage by borrowing the needed $1,500.00 in the event that my offer was accepted. The use of leverage is a real money-making principle, as I previously explained in Chapter "Six."

I encountered several surprises at the closing. First of all, the lady that conducted the closing was not the same one with whom I had been negotiating. She was the office manager who worked in that position only during the winter months. During the summer, she returned back to her home up north; in other words, she was a "snowbird." She obviously had little motivation to prepare and complete the enormous amount of paperwork necessary for us to receive ownership of the mobile home and a lease on the lot. Secondly, the mobile was represented as belonging to the "estate" of the deceased couple who formerly owned it. However, I soon learned that, according to the information on the contract, the owners of the park were then the actual owners of the mobile. Thirdly, there was a $300.00 "processing fee" added to my costs on the closing statement. When I questioned the fee, I was told that it was to cover the expense of the secretarial work necessary to complete the transaction. I questioned and considered all three concerns but decided to go ahead with the deal anyway. I didn't believe that it really mattered who did the paperwork or from whom I was really buying the home. At first, I strongly objected to the $300.00 fee being charged to me. I later decided that it was not that big of problem because I would just add it on to my asking price for the home.

My fourth, and perhaps greatest concern, was the required commitment to a lease on the lot for a minimum of twelve months. I had been informed that the monthly rent for the lot was $359.00 per month but was not told that an annual lease was required. My big concern about the lease was whether or not it could be transferred to whomever I sold the home. I was told that it could be transferred, providing that the transferee was approved by the park owners. Such approval meant that all applicants must be a minimum of 55 years old, pass a criminal background check and have a good credit rating. I too had to jump through all the same hoops before I was approved to purchase the home in the first place. As you can tell my now, that little deal became more and more complicated as it progressed. I concluded that the park owners had purchased the home from an estate in order to work some kind of a deal to resume the receipt of a monthly lot rent at that address. They knew that by selling it to me, they would start receiving the rent again. Therefore, they were not at all helpful to me during the process of reselling the home.

The home obviously had not been occupied for several months. The interior was dusty and needed a good cleaning. The exterior, however, was in need of a little more work. Two sections of the porch had screens torn from the frame, the exterior needed a good pressure-washing, and the lawn needed some general trimming and maintenance work. Fortunately for me, a retired gentleman neighbor on one side of the home did lawn maintenance work and the neighbor on the other side did pressure-washing. I repaired the screen and hired them to do the other jobs for a total of $285.00. They finished their work in only one day and I was therefore able to immediately place the home back on the market.

Both of the gentlemen became more friendly and talkative as the work progressed. I learned from them that the park actually owned several of the mobile homes that were for sale; and, that other owners in the park complained about the office staff attempting to sell a prospective buyer one of their own homes instead of processing the paperwork for a lease on the lot of someone else's mobile home. That of course was a big concern to me, knowing that any future prospective buyer that I got would have to be approved by the park before I could make a sale.

While the two gentlemen were completing their work, I developed a five-page website on the internet called "floridahomebyowner.com," for a cost of only about $150.00. That project was a challenge, a lot of fun and well worth the investment. The first page, or "homepage," welcomed the viewers and informed them that the mobile home was completely furnished, from an estate and that it was for sale by owner. The page included an exterior picture of the home and invited the viewer to click on the other pages for additional information and to view the interior pictures.

After totaling my costs to date and calculating my future expenses, I knew that I would have to sell the home for a minimum of about $9,100.00 in order to accomplish my objective of making a $3,000.00 profit. To allow for any possible unanticipated expenses and to provide a little room for negotiations with a prospective buyer, I decided to price the home at $9,950.00. I posted the asking price on my website, thereby launching my marketing campaign to sell the home. I also placed a small free classified ad on an online site called ocala4sale.com. It is one of many sites by the network usa4sale.net and the very best source for online classified ads that I have found. In addition, I paid for another small ad in the "Mobile Homes for Sale" section of our local newspaper. In both cases, I referred the readers to my website for more details about the home.

The combination of ads in conjunction with the website worked like a charm. I received an average of about six calls per day. Several of the callers inquired about "owner financing," but much to my surprise, approximately half of the callers asked, "What all is wrong with it?" After not selling the home for several weeks, that question caused me to remember a situation that I was involved in several years ago. A friend of mine, who was a construction contractor, had taken a home on trade for a new one in Lexington, Kentucky. He had tried for several months to sell the trade-in but was frequently asked the same question; "What all is wrong with it?" I was in the real estate business at the time and he asked me if I would take a look at it and advise him on what I thought might be his problem. He said that he obviously had it priced too high because he had not had any takers. I toured the home with him and learned that it was in outstanding condition, had a great floor plan and was in a prime location. When I compared the home to others that had recently sold in the area, I realized that his asking price was grossly low. I told my friend that I was of the opinion that prospective buyers thought that something was wrong with the home because it was priced so low. I advised him to raise the price $45,000.00 and place it back on the market. He did, and the home sold the next week for the asking price. As an old friend of mine would say, "If I'm lying, I'm dying!"

I realized that I had made the same mistake as my friend; I had priced the mobile home too low and people got the impression that there was something seriously wrong with it. After all, the ads were very impressive, if I must say so myself. Based on that conclusion, I added an additional $3,000.00 to the asking price. The number of calls continued, but so help me, I didn't get another single question about what was wrong with it after I raised the price to $12,995.00.

Three days later, a couple offered to pay the full asking price. I directed them to the park office for approval to be tenants of the park. I was told that they would learn in about three days whether or not they were approved. Over a week passed and not a word from anyone about the request. I called the office and was told that, "Oh, they were not approved." I asked why I had not been informed. The lady in the park office told me that she had "left a message" on the applicant's answering machine. When I called the buyers, I was told that they had not received such a call. Now keep in mind that these buyers had cash to pay for the mobile home. All this caused me to realize that the future of my deal was in the hands of someone who had no reason whatsoever to approve a buyer for our mobile home. The park owners had us obligated to a lease and they knew that they would be paid the lot rent each month. Approving a buyer for us would not benefit them in any way; it would only result in a lot of additional work for them.

Within two days, I received another offer to buy the home at our increased asking price. This time, I explained the situation to the buyer and advised him that he would have to be rather forceful with the staff in the park office if he hoped to be approved. He was just the type of gentleman that obviously did not easily accept "no" for an answer. He took my advice and applied for residency in the park. The office manager would be vacating her position within one week, moving back to her hometown. Now this is where I got my lucky break. The office manager and the buyer were from the exact same town up north. They knew many of the same former neighbors and had eaten at many of the same restaurants. I can't help but wonder whether or not he would have been approved had that not been the case.

This was a very successful deal resulting in a profit of $8,450.00 on my leveraged $3,000.00. After paying off my loan of $1,500.00, I then had a total of approximately $10,000.00 cash on hand for my next project. I believe that equals my $100.00 gift being multiplied one hundred times. However, I will never again buy a mobile home that is located in a mobile home park, regardless of the price. The park owners wield too much control over the situation. Also, many prospective buyers who must buy a home in the lower price range cannot afford the high lot rent along with the home payments. However, I would welcome the opportunity to buy one, at a good price of course, located in a mobile home subdivision. In a subdivision, as opposed to a park, the ownership of the lot is included with the mobile home.

I believed that the increasingly high cost of new custom-built home construction was resulting in a greater demand for low-cost housing such as mobile homes. An equal demand was generated in the 1970s when interest rates increased to the 20% range. I started a very successful retail mobile home business during that period. After a few years, the interest rates began to drop, resulting in a proportionate drop in mobile home sales. When the housing market again shifted toward custom-built homes, I closed the mobile home business. My reason for telling you this is to emphasize the point that I firmly believe it to be just as important to know when to get out of a business as it is to know when to start a business. Practically nothing lasts forever except the land that it sits on.

CHAPTER TEN

The Unknown Value of Real Estate

There are many price and value guides being published today. Most of the popular ones are very dependable and include everything from an antique hand tool to a million-dollar motorcoach. The primary reason that they are important is because other people also refer to them for the value of an item. Let us consider the Harley Davidson that I sold as an example. The NADA (National Automobile Dealers Association) listed the average retail value at $9,205.00. Now you can rest assured that anyone who was interested in the bike probably researched the value the same as I. The person from whom I purchased the bike probably also did the same thing; however, the influencing factor to sell in his case was his desire to sell it immediately. Therefore, he was willing to accept considerably less than the average retail value for it. The value of most, if not all, vehicles are very easy to determine and therefore becomes a rather mute point in negotiations for the buying or selling of such items.

The one thing that I probably like to buy and resell the most is real estate. Unlike most items, a parcel of real estate is always unique. After being in the real estate business for several years, as a licensed real broker and a licensed real estate auctioneer, I learned that an accurate establishment of real estate values is extremely difficult to determine, no matter how much experience you might have or how many certificates that you might have hanging on your wall that support the claim to be a real estate appraiser. The fact is, a parcel of real estate is worth the least that the seller will take and the most that the buyer will pay. Any opinions of value by anyone else are just that, opinions. Furthermore, such opinions are usually biased and are most certainly influenced by the experience, or lack thereof, of any person claiming to be an appraiser. In case you have any doubt about this fact, let me tell you the following couple of true stories.

When I was employed as the Assistant Superintendent of our school system, the School Board, acting on the staff's recommendation, voted to sell an old abandoned middle school, along with all the adjoining land of course. The state law required us to obtain at least two appraisals from two separate licensed, experienced and certified commercial real estate appraisers. These appraisals had to remain confidential until such time that a contract to sell was secured. Performing as the good little government employees that we were, we advertised for professionals to submit their proposals and fees for such an appraisal. Two certified appraisers were selected and their credentials were thoroughly checked out through the county and the state. Both appraisers went to work,

97

independently as required, and in about four weeks, had their rather thick

documents completed. Now are you ready for this? One appraiser stated that

the accurate value of the property was $800,000.00. The other appraiser

certified the value as being $400,000.00. Now see what I mean about opinions?

How would you like to have bought the school board's property for the lower

appraised amount and sold it for the higher appraised amount? By the way

these two appraisals are a matter of public record in the school board office.

To further illustrate my point, I decided to get a so-called "market analysis" of

one of our own properties. I selected the top four sales producing real estate

agencies in town; and then, the top agent of dozens in each of those firms. The

selected four agents worked in the business fulltime and appeared to be the most

ambitious of all. I told each of them that we were considering selling and invited

them to individual interviews for the purpose of considering them for the listing.

Based on their presentations, each had obviously done his or her homework.

Each agent presented a very nice and thorough packet of information, with

pictures, in an attempt to convince us that we should list our property with him or

her. Each one also presented a great deal of documentation to support their

recommended asking price for the property. Included were comparable sales in

the area, similar properties that were currently listed, similar properties that were

recently sold, similar properties that had sales pending, and similar properties

that had failed to sell during the listing periods. All the agents were members of

the local professional board for real estate agents and all obtained their

information from the same sources. Even with all the similar qualifications of the agents and the identical information available to each, the lowest market analysis presented was $179,900.00 and the highest was $240,000.00. I learned back in the woods where I came from to calculate the difference to be a whopping $60,100.00; a rather handsome profit if purchased at the low price and sold at the high price, wouldn't you agree? I had an investment of only $97,990.00 in the property that the agents analyzed for me. It certainly is not my intention to be critical of real estate agents or appraisers; I am only making my point that not even the fulltime experts can tell me what a property is worth with any acceptable degree of accuracy. By the way, I have retained those presentations and documents for future reference if needed.

I consider the difficulty of establishing the values of real estate to be a really great thing. Why, you might ask? Well because such difficulty results in varying opinions and lots of room for negotiations. I have learned to get several certified summary appraisals on property until I get one that is close to the amount I want it to be. So, it costs a few dollars, but in my opinion, well worth it. Debating value with a seller of a vehicle who is standing there with a copy of the latest value guide in his hand is not a smart thing to do. Debating value with a real estate buyer or seller is a smart thing to do because I will assure you that down deep inside, he or she does not really know the true worth of the property; especially if you are the one with an appraisal in your hand at the time. Now think about this for a moment and I believe that you will agree with me on the appraisal issue. Let us consider your house that you now live in as an example, or perhaps the one across the street or down the road from you. How much do you think it is worth? See there, I'll bet you can't tell me what it is worth within

ten to twenty thousand dollars. Oh, with some thought, you might come up with

an opinion but not a certain value that you would be willing to bank on. I have

learned to use these unknown factors in real estate values to my advantage and

I'm sure that by now you too have "seen the light."

CHAPTER ELEVEN

Everything Is Relative

There is one thing that I have learned for sure; everything is relative. Before determining whether or not something, or perhaps someone, is too fat, too skinny, too tall, too short or too whatever, I always try to first determine what "yardstick" I am using for the measurement. Let us consider, for example, a mouse that is 2 pounds overweight; now I believe that you will agree with me that such a sight could be called just plain awful! As a matter of fact, such a weird-looking creature would be good cause for any decent mouse-eating cat to beat up on his mother for teaching him to hunt such a scary blob of stuff, much less eat it. Now on the other hand, when a shapely middle-aged lady of ideal weight gains or loses 2 pounds, it doesn't stop her from being chased by any middle-aged, convertible sports-car-driving, gold-chain-around-his-neck, recently divorced male. As a matter of fact, he won't even notice the difference and couldn't care less. So you see, the significance of 2 pounds depends on how much there is in the beginning. In other words, if you were to ask the mouse and the lady what 2 pounds meant to them, I'm sure that you would get two completely and emotionally different answers; however, 2 pounds are still 2 pounds, right? Yea right, but very, very relative.

I refer to this principle of relativity, as it applies to business, as "relative profit to price ratio (RPPR)." No, this does not mean a cut of the profit in a business deal that goes to a lazy and dysfunctional relative; it means that there must be enough room between the purchase price and the selling price, of whatever it is that I am buying and selling, to include my profit objective without it really being noticed. In other words, I don't want the inclusion of my desired profit to result in the item looking like the overweight mouse.

As a comparison, and for the purpose of further explaining my ratio of relative profit principle, let us consider my first deal with the bicycles, and my fourth deal with the Harley-Davidson motorcycle. I made a profit of $1,500.00 on the motorcycle and the deal looked as good as the shapely lady to the buyer. On the other hand, had I tried to add a $1,500.00 profit to the $100.00 bicycles, they would have looked liked the overweight mouse. As you can see, the application of my business principle of "relative profit to price ratio" is just as important as the one of exponential growth, and therefore deserves this separate chapter devoted to the subject.

Chapter Twelve

The Brown Recluse Spider

By then, I was of the opinion that my next speculative investment should involved real estate in some way because of the higher price range needed to continue with my plan; after all, I then had $10,000.00 cash to invest. But also, I liked the fact that real estate values are very difficult to determine, as I have previously explained in Chapter "10." For the above reasons, I decided to get into the housing market by buying a good deal on real estate.

It seemed logical for me to focus on finding a mobile home lot to resale because I didn't want to invest all of my $10,000.00 plus borrow a lot of money to buy an averaged priced custom-built home. If I used all of my $10,000.00, I wouldn't have any money left to pay the interest while the project was being re-sold. Also, there are several mobile home dealers around that need land on which to place a buyer's home before they can close a deal. That fact in itself convinced me that if I could negotiate to buy a mobile home lot at a good price, I could capitalize on the mobile home dealer's salesmanship abilities and needs to work for me without having to pay them a dime. Free labor is a good thing, especially if you can use it to make a lot of money for yourself. Maybe if farmers prior to the time of Abraham Lincoln could have used this little technique to get clothing manufacturers to help them pick cotton, there would have been no need to import slaves or fight a civil war; just a thought.

I began my next fun-filled adventure by going on dual fact finding missions. I needed to update my knowledge of the mobile home industry along with all the current governmental regulations pertaining to the subject. I also began my search for information on mobile home lots. I learned that the mobile home industry hadn't changed much in the past 30 years. The homes were still being constructed on an assembly line in a factory, marketed on a retail sales lot and delivered on wheels to the buyer. The major differences that I noticed were the higher prices and the fact that the buyer no longer kept the wheels, axels and towing hitch of the home. These items were returned to the factory for use in the delivery of another new home. This was obviously a positive cost saving move.

Governmental regulations pertaining to the mobile home industry have significantly increased down through the years. I learned, for example, that a new building code for the construction of mobile homes was enacted in 1994. That code increased the "wind load" requirements for the design and construction of new mobile homes to be located in the state of Florida. As a result, those constructed after that date are more likely to withstand higher winds without much, if any, damage. The cost for such construction has been a little more, but,

104

has resulted in the homes being more valuable. Furthermore, mobile homes constructed before 1994 are difficult to get insured.

Regulations pertaining to the necessary utilities for a mobile home have always been a major concern and cost; the three major ones of course being water, electric and sewer. There are multiple governmental agencies that regulate the installation and use of utilities. Some of them include building, zoning, planning, and health departments. Even the visit to one of these offices can result in a pain in the neck. At one such office, I was greeted with a sneer by a lady, or perhaps I should say by someone who might have been a lady at one time, who should have been arrested for attempted intimidation. She said, "May I help you?" Yea, I know, that was the proper thing for her to say, but the way that she said it, she just as well have said, "What do you want stupid; I know the answers to all important questions and you had therefore better hurry because the rest of the world cannot continue to function without the benefit of my knowledge and time?" You too have probably visited a government agency at one time or another and therefore know exactly what I mean. Perhaps taxpayers need to replace such employees with robots and be given legal authority to bang them on the head with a ball peen hammer anytime one of them fails to smile and immediately make us feel like the valuable citizen that we are; just another thought that I had rambling around in my head. And by the way, we need to spray some kind smell-good stuff on the robots to make them smell better than some of the humans that they replaced; you think there might be a deodorant for robots, perhaps called "Smell-Em-Good 10W-40 Weight?"

The more that I researched the current codes and other requirements the more I realized that I didn't want to get involved with installing utilities on a lot. The "red tape" required to install and use a septic system, for example, were numerous, very time consuming and costly. Therefore, I decided that I would try to find a lot with all the utilities already installed and approved because anyone to whom I would want to sell it to in the future would obviously want to do the same. There are always a few improved mobile home lots around because mobile homes, unlike custom built homes, can be rather easily repossessed. Can you just picture the events resulting from a "repo man" repossessing a mobile home in the middle of the night without providing the occupants, including the dog and a "goosey" feline, an opportunity to vacate their "castle" before departing for parts unknown? I believe that the most hilarious vision, of the many possibilities, would be the family cat circling the walls with an occasional trip across the ceiling as the mobile home shakes and rattles down the darkened highway to parts unknown to anyone aboard. Sorry about that; I just had to let that thought out. Now while your devious mind embellishes and recovers from that scene, I will continue with the business at hand.

The best place to find an improved mobile home lot is in a mobile home subdivision, of course. You surely agree that an insignificant molecule, one of Betty's terminologies, probably could have figured that out. My first objective was to locate such subdivisions in my surrounding area; and then, rule out those that did not appeal to me. I received a lot of information on this subject from the mobile home dealers in our county. I was able to find all of the subdivisions on the county property appraiser's website. In all, I identified twelve developments that I decided to visit. By physically visiting them, I was able to judge each one according to my first impression, a judgment normally called "curb appeal" by real estate agents. I immediately ruled out the ones that had unpaved streets and a lot of unsightly "stuff" scattered all around; including the ones with old used tires on the roofs of the homes to prevent the wind from creating a moon roof in that dwelling of choice. I sincerely believe that this "tires-on-the-roof " concept was conjured up by a local tire dealer who came up with an ingenious way to get rid of old tires that he had replaced with new ones; just another useful business concept for you to ponder. After all, getting rid of old tires these days is very costly.

It was obvious that the undesirable subdivisions lacked sufficient deed restrictions; or perhaps the enforcement thereof. As I before said, I have always tried to place myself in the buyers' position before I purchase something for resale. In other words, I trust my first impression to be the same as that of any of my future prospective buyers.

My next step was to identify the desirable lots that I was interested in buying. That process took several days and a lot of driving. In all, I found about 35 such lots in the various subdivisions. After eliminating those that did not have installed utilities, I had only 17 from which to choose. Here again, I realized that the required time and process of buying are approximately 98% of the efforts involved in a profitable deal. When referring to a profitable deal of mine, an acquaintance once said to me, "You have got to be the luckiest person in the world." My response was, "Yea, the smarter I work, the luckier I get." If you have something desirable for sale, the actual "selling" part of the deal is easy; it is just a matter of waiting until someone comes along that really wants what you have to offer. This is where the "desirable" factor in buying becomes so important. Few people are aware of the thought and time that must be dedicated to the buying part of a profitable deal.

I mailed letters to all 17 owners of the lots that I had chosen, and in several cases, I also contacted them by telephone. I explained that I was not a real estate agent and that we only wanted to buy the lot for ourselves. For whatever their reason, a lot of sellers do not want to list their property with an agent. I also told all the owners that we were in a position to pay cash if they were interested in selling. I received only 3 responses to my inquiries. Two were from real estate agents and only one was from an owner. The owner that did contact us said that he was interested in selling his lot for $12,000.00. After some discussion and negotiating, he agreed to accept $10,000.00 cash for it. He said that the lot had an approved septic system, a well, and public water available. It was located in a rather nice subdivision with paved streets. I considered the offer to be a good deal, however, I also knew that I had better check with the governmental agencies to make sure that the utilities were in an acceptable and usable condition. It was obvious that no mobile home had been on the lot for several years. Boy, am I glad that I did my homework on that one. I learned that, although there was in fact a sewer system installed on the lot in 1983, it was used for only three years. The "lady," that I mentioned above, was obviously happy to inform me that in order to use the system, I would have to employ the services of a licensed septic system installation contractor to certify that it met all current requirements. She said that would involve the digging up of the septic tank and "applying for an inspection" by "her" department. She said that all the other parts of the system would have to be "checked and certified." Since the system had not been in use for approximately 19 years, I assumed it to be possible that tree roots had grown into the system, or perhaps the materials used at the time it was installed were deteriorated to the point that they could not be used. The "mouth-behind-the-desk" also informed me that if any of the neighbors had installed water wells that were within 75 feet of any part of the septic system on this lot, we could not receive a permit for the use of it. This, of course, meant contacting the neighbors to determine if and where any wells had been installed. To complicate things even more, the lot was only 75 feet wide to begin with. Therefore, if any neighbor had installed a well even in the middle of his lot, it would be too close to get approval to use the septic system.

There is more to the story; the same lady also informed me that I would have to pay an "impact fee" of $8,400.00 to the county because the septic system had not been in continuous use from the time that it was installed until the date that a new law was passed requiring such fees, blah, blah, blah. The deal became even more complicated and complex when I learned that the only person who knew where the well and septic system were located had died years before, that public water was available but the line was located on the opposite side of the street, and that a new concrete driveway entrance would have to be installed to county building code. Also the electrical system would have to be upgraded to current code and inspected for approval prior to use. By now you have probably guessed the outcome of the possible deal; I dropped it like a hot rock that had just landed from outer space. I then continued my search for an improved lot. I have always believed that if a deal is not simple and doesn't come easy, you best leave it alone. The moral of the story is, always do your homework and be extra cautious of believing what you are being told by anyone about anything that you are considering buying; whether it be for resale or personal use.

One day while driving through the same development, I thought that I saw a for sale sign on another vacant lot. The lot appeared to be about the same size as the one above that I told you about. I eventually purchased that one for $8,500.00 and resold it for $14,000.00; a profit of $5,500.00. As you are probably assuming by now, there is a lot more to this story, although it was really a rather smooth deal.

As you know, businesses come in all shapes, sizes and forms. The one that had this lot listed and advertised was a real estate agent that I would call, well, for the lack of a better description, an "original agent" of the community. I have no doubt that he was in the business when our town was just that, a town, rather than the city that it is today. He probably started his business in the same little office, which is attached to the side of a welding shop, that he is in today. To talk to a member of his staff, you have to talk to him; because he is the only member of his staff. That is, unless you want to consider his answering machine as being in the "staff" category. His answering machine has about the same personality as he; you just get the simple message, "Hello; leave me a message."

I have begun with the above explanation because it is typical of the several interesting observations and events throughout this transaction. To start with, the agents sign on the lot reminded me of a drop of water that was trying to be seen while tucked away in the middle of the Amazon rain forest; you just couldn't see it. Saying that the lot was overgrown is certainly a gross understatement. Anyway, I did observe what appeared to be a sign the first time that I drove by the lot. Sure enough, it was; all I had to do was tramp down a few weeds and bushes in order to get the message; no pun intended. Now, let's get serious here for a minute. The condition of the lot and the agents sign indicated to me that the lot had probably been on the market for a long time. Therefore, there was a good possibility that I could negotiate to buy it for a very good price, have it cleaned up and then resell it for a nice profit. Now the process of getting it "cleaned up" gets real interesting, but I'll tell you about that later. Sometimes these stories just jump out of order and get in the wrong sequence. But I promise to do my best to keep them in their place. I jotted down the number on the sign for future use. I later learned that, according to public records, the owner then lived in Michigan but had purchased the lot in 1970 for $400.00. I concluded that since he lived in another state and had owned the lot for the last 35 or so years, the old boy was probably very serious about selling. I have been trying to determine in which of my six "D" categories I would place this situation but I'm having a difficult time finding a slot for it. Perhaps it would be the "desperate" category because he was desperate to get rid of it before he died and the property was inherited by a relative who contributed to his demise in some way. Now there is a motivation to sell if there ever was one.

The lot was currently assessed, for tax purposes, at $5,760.00, an amount that is normally below the current market value by as much as fifty percent. All things considered, I concluded that it was worth a wholesale value of around $10,000.00 and a fair market value of about $13,000.00 to $14,000.00. Keeping with my policy of making my first offer below what I believe the seller might accept, I decided to offer him $8,500.00 for it.

Having experienced the difficulties with trying to buy the other lot in this development, I knew that I had better check out the requirements for installing a septic system on this lot. Once again, I am glad that I did. I learned the county and state health department code would not permit the installation of a new septic system on any lot that was only 75 feet wide; that is, without a variance being approved by the state. However, since there was a reasonable possibility that such a variance would be approved, I decided to make this subject one of the conditions of my offer.

I called the agent's office and got the short recorded message from his answering machine. I left my name and number as ordered. Later that day, he returned my call. I informed him of my interest in the lot and he told me that the seller was desperate to sell; now see there, I told you so. He said that the listed price was $15,000.00. Using my old "it might be worth it" tactic, I told him just that, that it could very well be worth that but I didn't have that much to spend on a lot. He then fell into my trap by asking me how much I did have to spend. I told

him that the maximum would be maybe $8,000.00, but no more that $8,500.00

for sure. I then explained my concern about not being able to get a permit to

install a sewer system on the lot. The agent said, "Well, I don't know if he would

go that low or not, but maybe he will. I will give him a call to see what he says."

He also told me that the owner had applied for the variance and a permit for a

sewer system; however, he did not know the status of that application. He then

said that he would see what he could find out and get back with me. Low and

behold, and much to my surprise, he called back in about ten minutes and said,

"We have a deal." He also told me that the request for the variance had been

approved. When my offer is accepted that fast, I get a sick feeling in the pit of

my stomach. I can't help thinking, "I offered too much; I bet he would have taken

a lot less." But the feeling soon passed and I decided that, what the heck, I'm

getting a good deal and I know that I can make it profitable as planned. I soon

had the deed and the permit in hand. I paid for it with $8,500.00 out of the

$10,000.00 that I then had on hand.

Now back to the story that I have been dying to tell you. As I said, the lot was

overgrown and was therefore in bad need of some bush-hogging. Now in case

you are not sure what a bush-hog is, I will first describe it to you by telling you

that it is not a four-legged animal that lives in the bush. Actually, it is a four-

wheeled tractor, and not a four-legged animal, that pulls a big ole mower, called

a bush-hog behind it. This mower has a big blade that goes round and around.

As it is dragged over weeds and bushes, it literally "eats" them and spits out little pieces wood in the forms chips and sawdust. I contacted this "character" that had such machinery and hired him to do the job. At first, I thought that perhaps I should refer to him as a "gentleman" because calling him a character might offend him. But what the heck, I'm calling him a character because the odds are real high that he will never even hear about this book, much less read it.

The character met me at the lot and agreed to do the mowing for $60.00. He told me that he would go home, get his tractor and be back in a little while. He later pulled up in an old beat-up truck that was pulling a trailer. The trailer was obviously too small for the big new tractor that he was hauling on it. Also, the mower was an old one that was so small that it looked like a hand type push lawn mower that was attached to the tail end of an elephant. He got out of the truck and I wondered, as I had before, what in the world had happened to his right arm. It was a greenish-purple color; for some reason, it reminded me of the arm of a Martian. It was all puffed-up and reflecting the sunlight like the hood of his new tractor. I couldn't stand it any longer so I asked, "Man, it looks like this bush-hog got you down and rooted you around for a while; what happened to your arm?" Now are you ready for this? He said, "Aw, I got bit by one of them damn 'reuse' spiders." After wallowing that statement around in the depths of my thought processes for a while, I finally concluded that he was talking about a brown recluse spider. I was having a heck of a time trying to determine the first use of a spider, much less a "reuse" for one. These spiders are rather common in the south and are very poisonous. Their bite doesn't necessarily result in death; it just makes the patient wish for death to ease the pain. They are sometimes referred to as "fiddleback" or "violin" spiders because of those shapes on their backs. One of the websites that I checked out on these little devils informed me that brown recluse spiders are called "recluse spiders;" now I believe that I could have figured that one out on my own, don't you? The man told me that right after he had been "bit," his wife used a snake-bite kit to "suck out the poison." He added, "Yes sir, I'm telling you my damn arm turned black and blue clean up to my shoulder. My old lady took me to the hospital and I thought I was going to die; but I didn't." Now see there, I told you that he was a real character; maybe the spider also messed up any logic that he might have once had because I could see that he wasn't dead. I was beginning to regret asking him about his arm because it wouldn't be long until dark and any mowing was looking questionable.

As he continued to talk, the story got even more interesting. He told me that his "little woman" was real good to him; that she was so concerned about him getting "bit or hurt" that she "took out" a real good life insurance policy on him. I got the strong impression that he didn't know the difference between an accident policy and a life policy. Don't you agree with me that he had better keep a close eye on his "little woman" to make sure that she doesn't see to it that another "reuse" spider bites him? She just might not suck out the poison next time.

He continued by telling me that, after he bought his big new tractor, he "figured out" that the mower was too small and that he needed to buy a "bigger" one. I agreed that his old and smaller tractor probably would have done the job since he didn't have a new and larger mower to go with the new tractor. He also said that he was having a problem with the tires on the trailer because they too were too small to haul the big new tractor. He said, "I have already 'blowed' out two of them." I also agreed that he needed new tires. I then asked him whether or not he thought his truck was big enough to pull such a big load. He said, "Naw, its not; I'm going to have to buy a bigger truck too." He said that he would have to get some more jobs in order to have enough money to buy anything else because it was taking all that he could "take in" to make the tractor payments. Now give that statement some thought if you want your ears to swap sides. Finally, he got the lot mowed and I paid him for his service.

I then witnessed what can happen when a good ole boy tries to load a big ole tractor on a little-bitty trailer with bad tires; in the dark. It was an absolute hoot; but I will save that story for another time. It is obvious that I could write another book about the gentleman after spending only a couple of days with him. (Now see there, I really am nice, I called him a gentleman.)

The purpose of this whole story is not to belittle that hard working gentleman, but rather to emphasize, in hopefully a rather amusing way, the importance of developing a good plan before going into any kind of business; and above all, don't get "bit" by a "reuse" spider or you too might have a price on your head.

Boy I sure have wondered from the main subject of this chapter, haven't I? Ok, I'll now get back on track. As I said, I bought the lot for $8,500.00. It was then time to decide on an asking price and begin advertising it for sale. I doubted whether or not I could double my investment this time, but I wanted to make at least a $5,000.00 profit on the deal in order to maintain the exponential growth of my original $100.00. Therefore, I added that amount plus 6% in the event that a real agent came along with a buyer and I needed to pay the agent a commission. I also added in a few hundred dollars for incidental expenses and income tax. The total came to $17,260.00, so I decided to price the lot at $17,500.00.

After the lot was on the market for a couple of weeks, Betty and I took a little trip up the east coast in our motorcoach. We had worked our way up to Philadelphia and were standing right next to the grand old liberty bell. The ranger was telling the crowd about the many battles that had been fought for freedom and the role that the bell had played in our history. He did such a good job that I felt as if I had regressed in time and was right there on the battlefield. All at once I felt a sharp sensation in my left side. I had a strong urge to yell out, "Medic, medic, I've been hit." But not to worry, I had not been shot. The only negative thing that happened was the puzzling stare that the ranger gave me in response to my muffled grunts. I was getting a call on my cell phone which I had programmed to the "vibrate" mode before entering the building. But of course, that was not the time or place to answer a phone call; especially when I was being stared at.

When we were again outdoors, I listened to the voicemail that I had received. The message was from a gentleman who said that he was interested in buying the lot. From some of his comments, I concluded that he was a speculator just like me. For one thing, he began by telling me that he was interested, but didn't have "that kind of money." I returned his call and, playing his game, asked how much he could afford to pay. He said, "The most that I can come up with is

$14,000.00." I told him that I was not sure whether or not we could "come that low" but that I would think about it and call him when we got back home. I knew that I couldn't do much else at the time while standing in the middle of Philadelphia with pee running down my leg as a result of my recent battle injury; just kidding. I got his phone number and we continued our trip.

When we returned from the trip, almost three weeks had passed. I have learned from experience that if a deal is not made within 24 hours after it begins, it probably never will be made. Therefore, I believed that under normal circumstances it would be a waste of time to call the man; however, in this case, I did call him again. It was obvious that he was anxiously awaiting my call. Later that same day, we met up, signed a contract and he paid me a $1,000.00 deposit. We closed the deal for $14,000.00 in about three weeks. I made a profit of $5,500.00, which exceeded my objective by $500.00.

About a week later, I drove by the lot to learn if my hunch about him being a speculator was correct. It was; there was a "for sale" sign on the lot with his phone number on it. I had a friend of mine call the number and ask the price of the lot. He was told that the asking price was $20,000.00, but that the seller would entertain a reasonable offer. Now I assumed as much, didn't you?

Over a year later, the lot was still for sale; and, in bad need of another bush-hogging. After giving it some thought, maybe the lot was again overgrown because the bush-hogging gentleman's "little woman" is now living high-on-the-hog," so to speak, off his life insurance policy. Remember my 6 "D's" that I told you about. My reason for selling did not fit into any of the categories, did it? I then had $15,500.00, which considerably exceeded my $12,800.00 objective, for

my next exciting project.

Chapter Thirteen

Kentucky Corn

I suppose that most people are not unlike Betty and me when it comes to the roots of our raisings. There are the remaining families, the many friends, the favorite places, and even the smell of our childhood homes that keep drawing us back in an attempt to relive the pleasures of the past. But of course, there are always some old painful memories that keep trying to creep into our emotions; however, the passing of time seems to help heal some of those old wounds a bit, but I believe that the deep scars are always there to constantly remind us of the many tears that we have shed down through the years. Even though we have been gone from there for many years, we always look forward to returning to our home state of Kentucky. We try to visit our hometown of Richmond several times a year. Every time that we return, it is like a homecoming week for an alma mater; we have an absolutely great time.

Upon arriving at those "old stomping grounds" a few months ago for a visit, I suggested to Betty that we might just buy some land there and prepare it to accommodate the parking of our motorcoach. Perhaps we could buy enough to permit us to sell off half of it and then have our half of it free. With that, we could go back to Kentucky whenever we wanted and stay as long as we wanted. We were, and had been for several years, staying in a very nice little campground located in Berea; which is only about 12 miles south of Richmond and just off Interstate 75. To my knowledge, there are still no campgrounds in Richmond.

After doing some shopping in one of the local food markets, I picked up a magazine on the way out. It was called, Madison Kentucky Homes Magazine. It seems that just about all the local real estate agencies advertised in that book. Upon thumbing through the pages, I came upon a very simple ad that stated:

"2 Acres – Cartersville. Harmon's Lick Road. Only 10 minutes from Berea & I-75. $16,500.00."

I called the agent and inquired about the exact location of the land; and then drove out for a look-see. I'm here to tell you that it was some on the prettiest land that I have ever seen. It reminded me of the rolling countryside of Germany. It was surrounded by acres and acres of bluegrass land and tobacco fields to the north and west. Just past the big farm to the rear were the magnificent mountains of the Daniel Boone National Forest. Adjoining the property to the right was a well-groomed civic park with a large pavilion, barbeque grills and ball courts. To the south and front were fields of freshly mown hay with the cattle grazing on the other side of the farm. I can still smell that freshly mown hay even today. The property had a nice paved road in front with a public water line plus a natural gas line in the ditch just off the pavement. A main electric line ran across the back side of the 2 acres. Remember what I said earlier about curb appeal, well now dear reader of these words, this place had fantastic curb appeal. I know that by now you are thinking, "I'll bet that the old boy bought this land."

I called the real estate agent and asked if she could meet up with me at her office to further discuss the possibility of buying the land. I told her that I would like to also have any information that she might have about the legal description, along with a plat of the property. She said that she would gather up everything and meet me at her office in about an hour.

Although the asking price of $16,500.00 appeared to be a pretty good deal, you know that I just had to make a lower offer, no matter how much I wanted the property. I really believed that I could sell one of the acres for around $12,000.00. Now all I needed to do was find out if one of my "D's" applied in this case, and if so, I might be able to buy the whole thing for $12,000.00, sell off one acre, and therefore accomplish my objective of having a one-acre lot for our use; free!

Now I would enjoy describing the lady that I met at the real estate office and would likewise enjoy telling you another story that would probably parallel the one about the character with the new tractor that I told you about earlier. But I won't because she looked like she might have read a book or two in her life. Appearance aside, she did seem to be professional in her dealings; after all, that is all that matters isn't It? I first asked her how long the property had been on the market. She answered, "Several months." I then inquired about the reason that the owners were selling. She said that the lady's parents had "cut off" the two acres for their daughter, and her husband at the time, to build a new house on. But, that they had gotten a divorce before they built anything. I tried not to smile but I was thinking, "Look-a-here, look-a-here!" After carefully studying the legal description and the drawing of the boundaries that she had, I determined that the 2 acres could easily be divided. One very important thing that I had to consider was the fact that the county there requires a minimum of one acre before a sewer system can be permitted. Therefore, I had to be absolutely sure that the 2 acres were in fact two full acres or more.

All things being considered, I made the agent an offer of $11,500.00. I told her that I could pay cash as soon as the sellers could make a deed to me. Now I learned a long time ago that the words, "fast cash" really gets the attention of a couple who recently decided to divide up their marbles and ride off into the sunset and in different directions; is that possible? Anyway, in response to my offer, the agent told me that the sellers really did want to sell but that she didn't believe that they would go that low. I then began my routine of not having any more money to invest in a single lot that far from town. I told her that, however, I could probably come up with another $500.00 if they did not accept my offer and if she thought that it would do any good. She said that she was willing to give it a try. I knew what she was thinking because I have been in her shoes many times before. She was thinking:

"I can tell them that the man said that he was not in a position to pay more

123

than $11,500.00; but, he won't have to go through the long process of getting

a loan and a mortgage because he has that much in cash. As you know, that

is the best offer that we have had. However, I believe that I can get another

$500.00 out of him, so I suggest that you counter his offer with $12,000.00 if

you really want to sell."

I can see it now; she would probably stand in front of the sellers with her chest

out and proud as punch while making her little speech. On second thought,

disregard that part about her chest sticking out; I don't believe that the impact of

such a vision can be conveyed in words.

The agent completed the contract and I signed it. We parted ways for the

day. The next day, she called me and said that the sellers were really hoping for

a better price, would not accept the $11,500.00 but under the circumstances,

would accept $12,000.00. How's that for negotiating? Almost 25% lower that the

listed price that was a good deal to begin with. And, they had to pay the agent

her commission out of their proceeds. Betty and I went to the closing with

$12,000.00 of the $15,500.00 accumulated to that date and then left with a deed

in hand. By the way, I had also negotiated for the sellers to pay for a title

insurance policy for us. In case you don't know what this is, it is a policy

guaranteeing that the title to the property is free and clear with no encumbrances,

other than those on public record. Should there later be a problem with the title,

the insurance company is responsible for the resulting costs.

In order to get the approval to install a septic system in that area, one must

hire a licensed engineer to perform what is called a "perc test" on the land. That is short for percolation and involves the digging of holes of a required depth and in various locations. Water is then poured into the holes and the engineer records the rate that the water "percolates" into the soil. If it percolates at the minimum required rate, a permit to install a sewer system may be issued. Being familiar with Kentucky soil, there is always a possibility that there is a layer of clay just below the surface that will prevent such percolation. In the process of determining exactly what I needed to do to obtain a permit, I learned from the local building department that the sellers had already had the test performed and that everything was "good-to-go." Another big "look-a-here, look-a-here!" I got a copy of the approval and with it, had another big selling point on my side. An acre of land with public water, natural gas, electricity, and an approval for a septic system for a measly $12,000.00; how could any prospective buyer go wrong with a deal like that?

Knowing that I would soon be headed back to Florida, I contacted a different real estate agent in town. I believe that you will agree that it wouldn't have been very wise to deal with the same one from whom we purchased the property. I can hear and see her reaction now if I had told her that we wanted to list the property for double that which we had just paid for it. She would have probably just said, "You want to what? Surely you gist." I told the different agent that I wanted $15,000.00 for the acre lot, but that if someone came along who wanted the 2 acres, I would let them both go for $25,000.00. She said that the price seemed reasonable to her and that she would be happy to work with me to get them sold. She said that however, there were several lots on the market that

125

were one acre or less in size. She highly recommended that we not divide the land but rather sell it as a two-acre parcel in order to be more competitive on the market.

Another thing that I started thinking about was the cost of improving the acre lot for our use. There would be the costs of the sewer system, water lines, electrical lines and hookups, culverts for the entrance, a driveway thick enough to support a heavy motor coach, etc., etc. There would also be annual property taxes to pay, along with a minimum electric bill each month. Then of course there would be the problem of keeping it mowed when we were not there. When I totaled all this up, I discovered that we could stay in the local private campground for several months each year for a fraction of the cost of owning our own lot. Needless to say, it didn't take me long to call the agent back and tell her to forget dividing the two acres. I told her that instead, to just list the property as a great two-acre parcel on a nice paved road and with all the utilities available.

Remember I mentioned that the neighboring farmers were cutting hay? On this subject, I received a phone call not long after the agent had installed her sign on the property. It was from our neighbors who owned the big farm that adjoined us to the rear and left side. He told me that his sister is the person from whom we purchased the land. He requested that he be permitted to keep our property mowed in return for the hay that it produced. It didn't take me long to agree to that proposition because I had been concerned about how I was going to keep the property mowed until it sold. This was one of those situations where it was a good deal for the both of us. With that, Betty and I headed back to Florida in our "mobile condo."

Several weeks passed and our agent did a great job keeping us informed about what was happening with the sale of our property. However, I don't believe that she made any more trips out there to visually check it out. As autumn approached, once again Betty and I started considering another trip back home to Kentucky. We wanted to get there before all the tomato crops were gone and to enjoy the autumn colors of the leaves. We had been talking about this to a couple of friends of ours, Carlene and Ellis. They too have a motorcoach and we invited them to go with us. They accepted our invitation and we began to plan accordingly. Ellis and I decided to take our motorcycles, which he refers to as "hogs," with us so that we could do some riding through the mountains of Kentucky. We loaded our bikes on Ellis's trailer and headed north; Ellis pulling the trailer and me towing my pickup.

I had told my motorcycle-riding buddy Ellis about buying the two acres in Kentucky and was anxious to show off the good deal to him. I was bragging about how pretty the land was and that I had a guy that was keeping it mowed for me while I was gone. I told him that it was so nice that we might just change our minds and build two RV pads and hookups on the property for the two of us to use.

The next day after we arrived at Walnut Meadow Campground in Berea, I loaded Ellis into my truck and we made the short journey to our country paradise. As I drove down the road, I realized that I had just passed the park that I told you about earlier. For a few minutes, everything started getting hazy to me as if I were in a cloud of smoke. I said, "Now wait a minute here, where in the heck is my land?" I knew that it was supposed to be to the left of the park, but I didn't see it. All I saw was a large cornfield on the adjoining farm. Then all at once it dawned on me that at least part of that cornfield belonged to us. Even though I was embarrassed, Ellis didn't rub it in too much; as a matter of fact, he was very kind to me. However, he did have a little fun with me after we returned to the campground and started telling the story to the ladies.

It didn't take me long to determine that the guy who was supposed to have mowed our property, had in fact planted and was growing corn on it. I thought that perhaps we would just take advantage of the situation and pick us some fresh corn for dinner that evening; after all, it was our land and I yearned for someone to come by and accuse us of stealing. I'm telling you, that corn was as hard as dry roasted peanuts. We were a week or two too late for the season.

Not knowing who to talk to about the corn, I asked the neighbor on the other side of the park whether or not he knew who owned the cornfield. He gave me their names and told me that they lived in the big house that could be seen way back on farm. I gave them a phone call and a woman answered. She was obviously the mother of the whole clan. After I explained the agreement that I had with her son to mow the land, I asked her how in the world it had gotten twisted around to become an approval to raise corn on our property. She told me that she had been by there and that whoever told me that they had corn on us was "flat-out lying." It didn't take me long to realize that she assumed that I was

128

in Florida and that they would have time to harvest the corn before we came back up to Kentucky. I'm telling you, I was so "hot under the collar" that both hairs on the top of my head must have been standing straight up. I fought back a strong desire to use a few choice words to express my frustration. Instead, I kept my cool and informed her that I was standing in front of the cornfield and that, in my opinion, they were guilty of trespassing. I told her that I was going to the local sheriff's office and file a complaint. She might have been the matriarch of the clan, but that got her attention. She told me where they lived and requested that I come to their home to talk to her. I wasn't about to do such a stupid thing as to place myself in a position like as that. I told her that I would be around for another 30 minutes or so, and if she wanted to talk, come to me and on our land. She then told me that she would have her son come talk to me. Now can you just see me standing in her front yard with a shotgun barrel peeping around the door at me? The business oriented moral of this story is to always negotiate on your own turf; not that of your opponent, that is if you expect to win the contest or perhaps not get shot in the process of trying to do so.

In about 15 minutes a very "healthy" looking young man pulled up in a beat-up old truck. He had a big chew of tobacco in his jaw and obviously had been working at some hard task most of the day; for a minute or two, I thought that he and Jed might be on their way to Beverly Hills. I didn't know whether to run or get mean. I decided to get mean; after all, I am an old man and could have him put in jail for attacking a senior citizen in case things didn't go my way. Ellis started easing toward my truck; I was only hoping that he wouldn't drive off and

129

leave me. Once I could have sworn that I heard him say that he was going for

help. But I wasn't worried because I knew that I could count on Ellis to stand

behind me; I just didn't know how far behind me he would be.

I used an offensive approach and told the man that he was only 15 minutes

from jail time. And, that if he couldn't give me a good answer to the question of

what he was going to do about the corn, I would still consider that as an option.

Well, it worked. I have never seen anyone so scared to be his size. After the

color returned to his face and he recovered the ability to speak, he simply asked

me what I wanted him to do. You think maybe his color could have had

something to do with the possibility of him swallowing the tobacco? I told him

that I would give him 48 hours to get the corn off my property and get it sowed

down in grass; otherwise, I was going the see the sheriff about issuing a warrant

for his arrest. I also told him that if he didn't get it done as I demanded, my

attorney was ready to sue him for the cost of having someone else do it, plus all

attorney fees and court costs. I then suggested that he would have a hard time

paying for all that if he was in jail. After I saw that I was winning, I pretended to

start getting angry, within reason of course. I asked him, "In Gods name son,

what in the world were you thinking? Where did you ever get the idea that you

can go onto another person's property, plow it up and plant corn for your

personal use?" He then told me that his older brother had said that I gave them

permission to raise the corn there. Although I was apparently winning, I wasn't

about to tell him that his brother was a liar because I know that "them there is

fight'n words" in that part of the country; and besides, I knew who would win if it came down to a fight. Being in my best interest to do so, I let that subject pass and asked him, "What will it be; are you going to get this stuff off my land or are you going to jail?" He said "I'll get it cleaned up next week;" to which I replied, "48 hours from right now, not next week!" He said, "Ok, I'll get it done one way or another," and with that, he cranked up his old truck and left in a puff of smoke.

Two days later, I drove back by the property and it was again recognizable; the crop was gone. My two hairs lay back down and I was satisfied; not happy mind you, just satisfied. I suppose that we could refer to this as my corn crop that never was.

Ellis and I spent the rest of the time that we were Kentucky riding through the mountains of that beautiful state. The weather was perfect, the leaves had just turned to all shades of gold and the smells of autumn were abundant all along the winding roads and by the silvery streams throughout the rides. There's nothing like the sound of a big ole Harley Davidson echoing off the mountains and through the hollows where a man spent his childhood days.

A few weeks after the corn matter was settled, the real estate agent called me and said that she had an offer of $15,000.00 for the two acres. I told her that, like I said, I would sell him one acre for that. She asked what would be the least that I would take for all the land. I said that I expected $25,000.00 but that if her buyer could come up with $24,000.00 for a fast deal, I would let him have it. She said that seemed fair and that she would see what she could do. The next day she called again and told me that she had a deposit from the buyer and was faxing a contract for us to sign. It ended up being a very simple transaction. We signed the agreement and faxed it to the buyer's banker. The banker called me and said, "Your check is in the mail." Since we are keeping score in this game of making money, I used $12,000.00 to earn $12,000.00; and did so without using leverage. With that, my total from the $100.00 beginning was then $27,500.00, surpassing my objective at the time by $1,900.00.   The deal in Kentucky proves that there are exciting adventures and opportunities wherever you might live or wherever you might roam in this great country of ours.

CHAPTER FOURTEEN

Improved Mobile Home Lot

My objective at this waypoint in my journey was to have parlayed my original cash gift of $100.00 into $25,600.00. However, successful negotiations had resulted in me having $27,500.00 instead. Perhaps if doubling the investment in each deal is called exponential profit growth, this could be called "super exponential" profit growth.

Another parcel of property that I had found was located in a different mobile home subdivision with very good deed restrictions. All the streets were paved and all the utilities were underground. The lot was completely improved with an electrical connection, a recently installed sewer system and a concrete driveway entrance that also had been installed to current county code. Rather than being only 75 feet wide, this lot was 100 feet wide by 120 feet deep. All the thousands of dollars in impact fees had already been paid and the lot was ready for a mobile home to be installed on it. I had estimated the value of this improved lot to be from $25,000.00 to $30,000.00. I learned, from researching comparable sales, that an unimproved lot in the subdivision was worth at least $19,000.00. I also knew that the cost for installing a septic system, electrical connections, water connections, and a driveway entrance at that time was approximately $10,000.00. Add to this the $8,400.00 impact fee and the total value could possible be a much as $37,400.00.

The lot had a real estate agencies' sign on it, however, I ignored it and wrote a letter directly to the owner. There is always the possibility that the agent's "listing" has expired and that I can therefore deal directly with the owner without having to indirectly pay a real estate commission. Apparently the listing had not expired because a few days later, the seller's agent called me. He informed me that his client was asking $22,000.00 for the lot. Now keep in mind that I had already done my homework and knew that he had paid $15,200.00 for it three years earlier. I thought that perhaps if he really needed to sell the lot, he would be willing to settle for the original cost plus the agent's commission of around $500.00. In keeping with my practice of making my first offer for an amount less that I expect the seller to accept, I told the agent that I could not pay the asking price but that I had $15,000.00 to invest in such a lot; and that if his client was interested, I could pay cash without the need for surveys, credit checks, loan approvals, and all the other "red tape" required by most buyers. The agent began telling me about all the improvements on the lot and that it was worth a lot more than I was offering. I told him that I was not questioning his reasoning, but rather I was simply informing him how much money that I had to invest in the lot.

Here as before, I avoided an argument with the seller involving the subject of value.

The real estate agent obviously complied with the legal requirement to inform his client about all offers because the seller called me the next day. He said that his agent was a close personal friend of his and that he had agreed to "drop out of the picture" so that we could deal directly. The seller told me that he had paid $15,200.00 for the lot, which I already knew of course, and that he would like to at least get his money back. He said that he was building a new home and the sale of the lot would place him in a position to complete the home without having to borrow any money. I agreed to buy the lot for that price, if, he would pay for the deed preparation and the title insurance; both to cost approximately $300.00. I also told him that, in return, I would pay for the state deed tax and the recording fees. He agreed and asked me, "Where do we go from here?" I told him that I could contact two or three local title companies and let him know what I found out. Fees charged by the various title companies ranged from $280.00 to $350.00. I informed the seller of my findings and faxed to him a simple purchase contract for his signature. He returned it, signed by him and his wife. I delivered the contract to the title company and we agreed on a closing date in approximately two weeks. My invested time paid off for me. I bought a very nice improved lot, priced at $22,000.00, for only $15,200.00; a simple deal with a minimum of invested time. I paid for it with money out of the $27,500.00 that I had accumulated. The minor closing went well and I was well on my way to making $50,000.00 from my $100.00 gift. Once again, the success of this deal proves that the accomplishment of a goal is simply the process of reaching a series of well planned objectives.

The closing went very smoothly. My closing cost was only $68.77, which I paid out-of-pocket. With a deed and a title insurance policy in hand, I began my advertising campaign to resell the lot. My first step in the process was to carefully arrive at an asking price. Now like it or not, life is made up of a series of competitive events. We compete with other applicants for jobs. People, with the help of health care professionals, compete with diseases in order to live a healthy and long life. Countries compete for foreign trade advantages. Businesses throughout the world compete for customers. Although I am not a big sports fan, as you have probably concluded by now, I am fully aware of the fierce competition in such situations. I am, however, a big fan of business and get a big kick out of making a sale to a buyer who has shopped my competition. I have learned that much care and time must be devoted to pricing anything for sale. I want to make sure that my price is at or below that of my competitors. I understandably want to make as much profit as possible, but at the same time, I don't want to leave a lot of money "on the table."

Before attempting to arrive at an asking price for the lot, I again researched the records of actual sales in the subdivision. This is known as the "comparable sales" approach to establishing value. A seller can ask whatever he or she wants, but unless a sale is made, the asking price has very little actual meaning; unless, the supply is very limited and the demand is very high. Fortunately, that was the case in this project. The subdivision was nearing completion to the point that only a few lots were left for sale. There were five unimproved lots (no utilities) owned by one gentleman and there was one other improved lot for sale. I called the owners and inquired about their prices. The gentleman with the five unimproved lots was by then asking $25,000.00 each for his. The lady who owned the one improved lot was asking $29,900.00 for hers. It is very important to note here that I had also performed all the research on values prior to buying the lot and therefore knew that I should be able to double my $10,000.00 investment. Inflation certainly worked in my favor during the short time that I owned the lot. I could then add my $10,000.00 profit objective to my purchase price of $15,200.00, plus, and additional $4,300.00 and still be priced $400.00 under my competition for a similar improved lot in the development. The additional profit provided me with a considerable amount of "wiggle room." It would permit me to pay a 6% commission if an agent happened to sell the lot; or, to reduce the price a little for that approximately 18% of buyers who must negotiate a price downward before they will buy. I placed a for-sale-by-owner sign on the lot and began advertising it at an asking price of $29,500.00.

An online classified advertising firm provided me with the opportunity to advertise the lot in four cities within central and northern Florida. The actual 400 character 30-day ads were free; however, I purchased a red border around each for only $3.00 per ad. The four ads read as follows:

"IMPROVED MOBILE HOME LOT for sale by owner. Septic system, electric, water, and concrete entrance already installed. Impact fees have been paid. A freshly mowed 100' x 120' lot ready for your doublewide NOW. Avoid the months of permitting, construction mess and thousands in impact fees. Near The Villages in Belleview Hills Estates, Summerfield. $29,500.00 for fast sale." (Contact phone number and email information were included at the end of the ad.)

The first response that I received to the sign that I placed on our lot was from the gentleman who owned the other five lots that he had for sale in the subdivision. By the way, my records show that approximately 80% of all the real estate that I have sold down through the years was the result of a for-sale sign being posted on the properties; not from advertising in the media. After asking for the price of ours, he informed me that he would "let his go" for $25,000.00 each. I did not tell him that we had previously talked or that I already knew the price of his lots. I simply reminded him that his lots did not include any improvements and that I was therefore not interested in them at the time. I said that I would give it some thought and perhaps get back to him at a later date. Opportunities for profits come and go, therefore, I always like to leave a seller with the positive thought that I might still buy whatever it is that he or she has for sale.

During the last part of the year of 2005 and during the first part of 2006, real estate values increased at an unbelievable rate. In order to keep up with the escalating prices, I found myself increasing the asking price of our lot by approximately $1,000.00 per month. Over a period of time, I increased the asking price from $29,500.00 to $36,900.00, for a total increase of $7,400.00. Guess what; yea, you're right, I sold it for the full asking price, a whopping

$21,700.00 profit. Now think about this for a moment. Once again, I accomplished my objective of an exponential growth profit; plus, an excess of $1,700.00. This deal further reinforces my belief that selling is a sport not unlike that of fishing; success is only a matter of keeping your hook baited and waiting until a "fish" comes along that wants that which you are offering. I believe that many sellers price whatever is it that they have to sell, and then reduce that asking price several times until it sells at a bargain basement price. They do this because they believe that a sale is not successful because the item is priced too high. Not true; if it was fairly priced, it didn't sell because a "taker" didn't know that it was in the water. Waiting for a "bite" requires confidence and patience. A friend of mine once said, "That is why it is called fishing; otherwise, it would be called catching." Have you ever noticed that fishermen who catch a lot of fish spend a lot of time fishing? I recommend that those without self-confidence and unlimited patience not get involved in the business game of buying and selling for a profit; or fishing for that matter. I'm sure that the little calculator in your brain has been clicking away and shows that my $100.00 gift plus profits now totals $31,700.00; not bad for a hillbilly from the woods, huh?

CHAPTER FIFTEEN

The Supply and Demand Factor

During the time that we owned the lot that just sold for $36,900.00, I had given the real estate agent a verbal offer of $21,500.00 on the only other improved lot in the development, which she had listed for $29,900.00. This was the same lot that influenced me to price ours at $29,500.00 in the beginning in order to give us a little competitive edge, yet, not leave much money "on the table." I also knew that if we could buy our competitor's lot at a reasonable price, we could not only make a profit on it, but more importantly, we would control the market for improved lots in that development. Therefore, we could raise the price of the lot that we already owned, as well as the other if we could buy it. I didn't believe that the seller would accept such a "low-ball" offer, but did believe that perhaps we would receive a reasonable counter offer. The agent had informed me that the sellers were having "some marital problems" that I considered being an important factor in making an immediate cash sale attractive to them. My objective was to take advantage of the "supply and demand factor" by controlling the supply. Considering the rapid growth in the area, I realized that the demand for low-cost housing already existed. Therefore, controlling such a limited supply should prove to be very financially rewarding.

A timely message from the real estate agent informed me that the sellers would not accept my offer of $21,500.00 but that they would take $25,000.00 cash, which was approximately 17% off the asking price. Well now I'm not the fastest hotrod on the track, but it didn't take me long to take advantage of the opportunity by being the first to leave the starting line. Within the hour, I had contacted the agent by phone. I told her that I really didn't want to pay that much for her lot. I asked if she thought that there was any possibility of the sellers accepting $24,000.00. She said, "Absolutely not," and obviously was not interested in taking even a lower offer to the sellers. By the tone of her voice, I believed that to be the case. I then informed her that we would take it at $25,000.00. We made arrangements to sign the contract and established a tentative closing date.

In the same email message, the agent informed me that another improved lot in the development had sold for $31,500.00 a few weeks earlier. Once again considering the current rate of inflation in real estate prices, I decided to change the asking price of our lot. Another factor that worked in our favor was the fact the county impact fees increased from $2,400.00 to a whopping $8,400.00 while we had the lots for sale. That, of course, resulted in our lots being worth an additional $6,000.00 each. Also, this second lot was larger that the first lot, which would therefore accommodate a larger mobile home.

With all things considered we priced the second lot at $39,900.00; which was $3,000.00 more than we received for the first lot. It took a little longer to sell this one because of the increased amount of money that the buyer had to borrow. When a $40,000.00 lot is added to the $80,000.00 to $90,000.00 cost of a large four bedroom doublewide mobile home, qualified buyers are few and far between. However, it did sell for the full asking price, which was a profit of $14,900.00, and we therefore had parlayed the $100.00 cash gift into $64,100.00 cash in the bank, exceeding our originally established goal by $12,900.00. I believe that we could call this another super exponential growth profit which resulted from taking advantage of the supply and demand factor in business. Am I proud of the fact that I accomplished my goal? You darn right I am; wouldn't you be? However, perhaps the pleasure that I received from writing this book gave me a greater satisfaction.

Chapter Sixteen

Free Stuff – Plus a Profit

Until now, I have shared with you some of my business principles and

concepts that I have used only after retirement. In doing so, I have demonstrated

what can be done with just $100.00. In this the last chapter, I would like to demonstrate to you how the application of my same principles and concepts previously used in this book can result in having just about any materialists thing desirable; without having to spend even one hard-earned dollar to do so, and in most cases, make a handsome profit in the process. I will tell you about a few of my adventures down through the years to prove that this is not only possible, but also show you how it was actually done. I shall then end this chapter with the profitable events that occurred to my benefit just last week. But before continuing, I would like to once again emphasize the importance of not becoming emotionally attached to or keeping the "stuff" that you buy and use while it is on the market for sale. Remember that such stuff is made everyday and that the next boat, car, motorcoach, airplane, or whatever, will be even prettier, faster, newer, better, and more desirable to both you and your future buyer. It is kind of like getting a younger and prettier wife every year. But of course, I would not know about this because I have had the same one for fifty years. Also, never forget the importance of negotiating for the right price and buying the most popular and desirable whatever-it-is.

For many years, Betty and I have enjoyed living in nice and comfortable homes, driven Cadillac's, ridden expensive Harley Davidson motorcycles, flown our own airplane, cruised the gulf in pleasure boats, traveled to many countries, and toured all of our great continental United States, several times as a matter of fact, in luxurious motorcoaches – ALL FREE! We did it by simply applying the business tactics that I have previously described in this book. I'm sure that most of our friends and families have often wondered how in the world we could afford such luxuries on teacher's salaries. Well, come travel with me now as I take you down the road of plenty. It is my road paved with the simple activity of buying something that you want and using it while waiting for it to resell; that my friend is my big "secret." And in most cases, I did it using other people's money, not mine. Now tell me, is there anything complicated about the concept? No there isn't; it is so simple that I can't understand what you are waiting for to apply it to your well-being.

While living in Florida and working for salaries in the mid 1980s, Betty and I had a burning desire to take a trip west. We wanted to see the Grand Canyon, Petrified Forest, Yellowstone National Park, the high country of Montana, snow on the mountains of Glacier National Park, and all the other sites to behold in our great land. But the problem was the fact that we couldn't afford it on our salaries. Now I have always believed in the concept that where there is desire, there is a way. With that in mind, I established the goal of a nice trip west with all expenses paid. I told Betty about my goal and she said, "Yea right; dream on dreamer." That statement only encouraged me because I know that a dream cannot come true unless it is in fact first dreamed. Here was my plan; negotiate for a good deal to purchase of a motorhome, borrow the money to buy it, use it for our trip west, and resell it for a profit to cover our expenses.

Unfortunately for the lady, she had recently become a widow and could not drive the motorhome that she and her recently deceased husband had enjoyed. It was a class "C" Chevrolet. In case you are not familiar with the classifications of motorhomes, a class C is the type that has the sleeping area over the truck

145

cab. Such little motorhomes are usually about 25 feet long and come equipped with a full kitchen, bath, shower, microwave, television, and many of the other comforts of home. This being exactly what we needed for our trip, I proceeded with my process of buying the unit.

Knowing that her reason for selling fell within the definition of one of my "Ds," as previously defined in Chapter "Eight," I decided to make her an offer of $12,000.00 for an RV then worth about $16,500.00. Knowing that she was not in a very good mood to start with, I was hesitant to make such a low offer verbally, so I wrote the amount on the back of one of my business cards that I had printed and handed it to her. I was thinking that if she wasn't then interested in my offer, she might become so later on. With my name and phone number, she would know how to contact me. Well, did that offer ever get her dandruff up; she started yelling at me in a voice so high that even today, I have no idea what she was saying. When her raving subsided a little and she started speaking more plainly, I definitely got her message when she said, "Get off my property, now!" In order to get out of the yard, Betty and I had to exit through the same gate used to enter her driveway in the first place. Wouldn't you just know it, the darn latch on the gate got hung against one of the side rails and I couldn't get it open. I found a low place in the fence to the right of the gate and went over it. I then grabbed the bottom of the fence so that Betty could scramble under. Not knowing what lay in store for us if we stayed in that yard much longer caused us to high-tail it to my pickup, get in and back up in reverse for about a half block. I felt that it was important that I knew where that woman was at all times while we made our escape.

After about three weeks had passed, I received a phone call from the lady that ran us off. She asked if I was still interested in her motorhome and whether or not I would be willing to give her $14,000.00 for it. I had assumed that this might happen because a motorhome is not something that sells very fast. I told her that I was not interested and that I had just about changed my mind about buying one at all. I continued by telling her that I always try to keep my word and that I would however still give her $12,000.00 for it because I said I would. Then in a very mellow tone of voice, she asked if I would pay her with a cashier's check. I told her that I would and we worked out the details for a closing from there. Borrowing $12,000.00 with which to buy the home was no problem because that was well below the wholesale value for it. We got the unit home, shinned it up right good and stocked it up with goodies in preparation for our first trip west.

We traveled westward across the lower part of the United States and ended up in San Diego, California. We then traveled up the coast of California and through the Redwood Forest to Washington State, eastward back across the middle states, and then southward back to Florida. It was a wonderful trip and I could write another book about our adventures. I know, this is not the time or place for that; however, you know that I must tell you about at least one little episode that comes to mind.

During the time of our trip, people were just starting to keep pigs as pets. Well now, we didn't know about such an interesting desire by some to have a pet pig. We stopped at a little roadside park that had a path leading up to the outhouses. Now notice that I said "outhouses," not restrooms. It was about 10:00 AM and I was having a snack; of all things, pork rinds. Well I'm telling you, I then witnessed something that I never even thought of happening. The pig that the woman was leading up the path stopped and had a bowel movement right there beside the path. Watching a human being leading a pet pig was one thing, but when she took out a tissue and wiped its behind, my snacking stopped right then and there; I just couldn't help but wonder whether or not the woman had eaten bacon and eggs for breakfast that morning. Now think about that for a minute and then catch up with me. As a matter of fact, I cannot to this day eat pork rinds; that scene of the pig all humped up with its tail being wiped is once again refreshed in my mind every time that I even think about pork rinds, much less try to eat one. At times, I even have to think about something unrelated before I can get bacon to go down the ole hatch.

Well, enough about what happened along the way on that trip; let us now continue with the business at hand. Fuel wasn't very expensive during that time and campground fees were in the $10.00 to $12.00 per night range. All of our expenses, including food, totaled $3,200.00; which wasn't bad for five weeks on the road. Since I had paid $12,000.00 for the motorhome, I needed to sell it for at least $15,200.00 in order to break even. Without going into a lot more detail about this, I will tell you that, after some negotiations, I sold that motorhome for $15,250.00, which was then about $750.00 below the retail value. Another big "Look-a-here, look-a-here" to you! I not only accomplish by goal, I made $50.00

148

in the process. Hope you enjoyed this yet another true story about how to have anything that you want – free!

Now let me tell you about our pleasure boat deal, and then I will summarize a few more examples of how to live "high-on-the-hog" for nothing. Living in Florida has a lot of advantages; one of which is the opportunity to enjoy the tropical settings on the Gulf of Mexico. That is of course, if you have a nice boat in which to do so. Remember what I previously said about buying the best of anything, and ensuring that it is the one that is most desired? Well, I followed my own advice and learned that a Hurricane brand boat, called a "Fun Deck," was the number one selling boat in the country at the time. Therefore, I began my search for such a boat. I found one with a 90 horsepower Mercury motor on it, and included a trailer, for sale by a boat broker in Flowery Branch, Georgia. Now in case you don't know where Flowery Branch is, it is a very nice little town east of Atlanta. To further refine the location, it is very close to Social Circle, Georgia, home of the famous Blue Willow Inn restaurant. This is a restaurant that serves home style cooking and sweet iced tea fit to die for. I never have any problem getting Betty to go with me to Georgia as long as I promise to again take her to the Blue Willow Inn.

The boat had very few hours on it and was in excellent condition. It had been repossessed by a bank in the area and the lenders had contracted with the broker in Flowery Branch to sell it. Once again, the reason for the seller to sell was one of my "Ds;" namely, "debt." I found the boat online and was able to negotiate for it in an open and fair manner. The current average retail value of the outfit at the time was $12,310.00; however the boat was in well above average condition. I was able to negotiate for the purchase price of $9,000.00, subject to my inspection and approval of course. After obtaining the loan and a cashier's check for that amount from my bank, Betty and I headed to Flowery Branch in our motorcoach.

The first night on the road, we stayed in a campground just south of Atlanta. The next day, we budgeted our time to ensure that we were at the Blue Willow Inn in time for lunch. Afterwards, we headed over to Flowery Branch. When we arrived, I saw the boat "standing tall" on the broker's lot. It was shiny white with blue trim and upholstery. The motor looked as if it has never been used. Neither the boat nor motor had ever been in salt water; just in a big fresh water lake in the area. Needless to say, I was happy with the purchase.

I hooked the boat and trailer up to the hitch on our coach and headed south back to Florida. When I got back home, I again checked the boat out thoroughly. It was in absolutely perfect condition. The next day, we headed over to the Gulf coast for our trial run. No problems, it ran and handled perfectly.

Remember I said earlier that the outfit had an average retail value of $12,310.00? Well I liked the boat so much that I put it back on the market for $13,450.00. Needless to say, I was obviously not in a hurry to sell it. As expected, it didn't sell for almost exactly 1 ½ years. Meanwhile, we used the boat a lot and enjoyed it tremendously. However, after that long, I was beginning to get tired of it and was ready to move on to something else. Therefore, I lowered my asking price to $11,950.00. After some further negotiating, and to make a long story short, I soon sold the boat to a gentleman in Orlando, Florida for $11,500.00.

Now see what I mean? I used other people's money to enjoy a fantastic pleasure boat for 1 ½ years at absolutely no cost to me except the approximately $900.00 interest; which by the way, I paid for out of the $2,500.00 profit that I made on the boat. I then had $1,600.00 cash as my reward for providing other kind, hard-working and money-depositing type people the opportunity to serve me. How's that for a deal? I'll bet that you're thinking, "You know, I believe that I can do that!"

Now here are few more examples of deals as promised. I decided that I wanted to learn how to fly an airplane; and I did. After earning my pilot's license, I wanted my own airplane; bet you could have guessed as much, right? I headed north out of Florida, stopping at every little airport along the way in search for an airplane that I could buy. I found a low-wing type Beechcraft at a little executive airport just west of Atlanta, Georgia. Have you noticed that the Atlanta area just seemed to be a "hot spot" for me to buy some stuff? It was a nice little plane with very low hours on it; an airplane that I knew would easily resell at any time. It was only about 6 years old; and besides, airplanes are well maintained in accordance with FAA rules and therefore don't normally depreciate very much from one year to the next; that is after the first year of course.

I learned that the owner of the airplane had unfortunately suffered a heart attack and therefore had to relinquish his pilot's license. I'll bet that you have concluded by now that this falls right into one of my "D" categories; well, you're right, its "disability." I'll just skip all the details about the negotiations and simply tell you that I purchased the airplane for a real good price.

Since airplanes do not have hitches with which to tow cars, I had a problem. There I was a long way from home driving a car and at the same time and place, was the proud owner of an airplane that I was not certified to fly. You see, I had my pilot's license at the time but I had not been "checked out" in that type aircraft. I realized that it would be very expensive to hire a pilot to fly the plane home for me. I thought to myself, now there has to be a way that I can get someone to provide this service for me without charge. After giving it some serious thought, I developed a plan and put it into action. I asked a couple of the local flight instructors if they had any student pilots that needed some cross-country flying time for certification. One of them said, "As a matter of fact I do." I told him that I had a win-win proposition; that if the student would fly my plane home for me, I would pay for the gas plus buy him a commercial plane ticket for a flight back to Atlanta. The instructor said that it sounded like a good deal to him, so he called the student. We made the deal and arranged for me to meet him at our local airport with the commercial ticket. Two days later, I witnessed my plane descending from the clouds and lining up for our runway. After he landed and taxied up to the tarmac, I gave him his ticket, dropped him off at the terminal and wished him a safe journey home. A neat thing to remember here is that a little thought and a well executed plan can get you free services as well as free stuff. I flew that airplane for 2 ½ years, got tired of playing with it and sold it for exactly

$70.00 more than I paid for it. Now that's what I call, "Flying high and free as a bird."

I mentioned before that Betty and I like to go back home to Kentucky every chance we get. The last time we went, I towed my motorcycle trailer, with the motorcycle in it of course. Knowing that we would not have a car to drive when we got there, I called one of my best friends, Kenneth, and suggested that he find us a car at a good deal. I told him that I would "put up" the money to pay for it, that Betty and I could use it while there, he could then resell it on his car lot, and that he and I could split the profit. Now I'm not too keen on any kind of partnership, but Kenneth and I have been best friends for many years and we both know that there is absolutely no way that either of us would attempt to be anything but completely honest with each other.

In a few days, Kenneth called me and said that he had found a nice Mercury for us. The seller wanted, to the best of my memory, around $2,500.00 for it. I ask Kenneth to see if he could get it for $2,000.00. The seller would not accept my offer but agreed to take $2,250.00 for it. I sent Kenneth a check to pay for the car.

When we arrived at the Berea campground, I couldn't believe my eyes. Kenneth was right; it was an exceptionally nice car. We drove it the entire month that we were there. As a matter of fact, we put a little over 3,000 miles on it during that time. Needless to say, the tires rarely had time to cool off before we and others were off in it again.

Before Betty and I headed back to Florida, we took the Mercury over to Kenneth's lot in Richmond. Kenneth and I agreed to ask $4,900.00 for it; after all, the book value for it at the time $6,050.00. About only a week or so had passed after we got back home when I received anther call from Kenneth. He said that he had a buyer who had made him an offer of $3,000.00 for the car. I suggested that he hold out for $3,900.00 for a response. The gentleman took it at that price. Kenneth and I split the $1,900.00 profit. In summary, Betty and I drove the heck out of a very nice and comfortable car for a little over a month and was paid $950.00 to do it. How about that?

I could go on and on telling you about similar deals down through the years that have provided us with the free use of just about everything that we have wanted. These are just a few that came to mind. Remember that I told you that I would end this chapter by giving you the details a couple of deals that happened just last week? Well here it comes.

Betty and I will be proudly celebrating our golden wedding anniversary in just a little over two weeks from now. We now own, free and clear, a luxury diesel motorcoach that... well now come to think of it, its probably in my best interest that we not go there now; perhaps that's a story to be told in private at another time and place. Anyway, Betty and I have been planning a two-month-long trip up the east coast, spending several days around New York City and then cruising on up the coast to other parts not yet decided. We have made the trip before, but want to take a little more time in doing so than we did before.

Up until about a couple of weeks ago, Betty kept asking me, "Donald, are you sure that we can afford to take our trip with diesel costing over $4.00 a gallon?" We can, of course, but she, the same as I have gotten accustomed to not paying for much out of our coffers. Back home, we called this "spoiled rotten." To set her mind at ease, I told her that I would "turn a deal or two" and make enough money to pay for our trip. I don't believe in spending time fretting over something that I can't do much about, like fuel prices; but I do believe in taking a positive action that is within my ability to alleviate the concern. Last Sunday, I began my search for something to buy for that purpose. I looked online at motorcycles and automobiles. I responded to about 20 different ads by telling the sellers "how much money I had" to buy one of whatever they were selling. The end result was that I purchased a 2004 Honda motorcycle and a 2000 Cadillac SLS. Both were in outstanding condition with very low miles. I resold the motorcycle in two days and made a profit of $1,000.00 on it. I then resold the Cadillac in 5 days and made a profit of $2,700.00 on it. Using the principles, concepts and tactics that I have explained in this book, I made $3,700.00 cash to pay for our trip.

I believe that this is a very good place to end this chapter, and this book as a matter of fact, so I will "shut up" for now and get on with my next goal of parlaying my $64,100.00 into $100,000.00; after all, I should be able to accomplish it with two or three more deals, don't you agree? Or perhaps I will call myself "The Negotiator" and start a business of negotiating for clients in return for a cut of the savings that I earn; who knows for sure what the future holds?

I really wish that there was a way you could come along with me to share in the joy and excitement of my journeys. That probably not being possible, I will end by saying that I truly do hope that you have enjoyed this book as much as I have enjoyed writing it; and that you can use my experiences as a guide to improve your life; at least in some small way.

I HATE TO TAIL YOU THIS, BUTT THIS IS THE END

www.ingramcontent.com/pod-product-compliance
Lightning Source LLC
Chambersburg PA
CBHW022057210326
41519CB00054B/600